THE GOLDEN TICKET

THE GOLDEN TICKET

A Life in College Admissions Essays

Irena Smith

SHE WRITES PRESS

Published 2023
Printed in the United States of America
Print ISBN: 978-1-64742-464-0
E-ISBN: 978-1-64742-465-7
Library of Congress Control Number: 2022913654

For information, address:
She Writes Press
1569 Solano Ave #546
Berkeley, CA 94707

Interior Design by Tabitha Lahr

She Writes Press is a division of SparkPoint Studio, LLC.

Some of the material in this memoir appeared in earlier form in *Mama, Ph.D: Women Write About Motherhood and Academic Life* (May 2008) and on *literarymama* (Jan. 10, 2010 and June 2014).

Names and identifying characteristics have been changed to protect the privacy of certain individuals.

"But there was one other thing that the grownups also knew, and it was this: that however *small* the chance might be of striking it lucky, *the chance was there*. The chance *had* to be there."

—Roald Dahl, *Charlie and the Chocolate Factory*

AUTHOR'S NOTE

The events described here are true to the best of my recollection (memories are imperfect things, after all). And while I've changed some names and blurred some identifying details to preserve confidentiality, I've adhered to the emotional truth of my experience throughout. All personal flaws and grammatical errors are, of course, my own.

INTRODUCTION

On March 12, 2019, the US government unsealed indictments against fifty parents who had collectively paid over $25 million to a college admissions consultant who guaranteed their children's admission to selective colleges and universities under false pretenses. The indictment unleashed a furor of frothing indignation, finger-pointing, and schadenfreude. The *Atlantic* published an article by a former college counselor at an exclusive Los Angeles high school eviscerating the college admissions system and powerful, entitled parents addicted to "the crack pipe of Harvard"; the *New York Times* crowed that the scandal laid bare "the elaborate lengths some wealthy parents will go to get their children into competitive American universities"; a former admissions dean wrote in *Vox* that the hysteria over highly selective colleges was fed by the *U.S. News & World Report*, whose rankings were nothing but "capitalistic undertakings rooted in junk science." And Elizabeth Warren said in an interview that the scandal represented just one more example of how the rich and powerful "know how to take care of their own."

But the truth is that all of us have a clutching need to take care of our own. I know because I work as a private college admissions counselor in Palo Alto, California—epicenter for off-the-charts parental aspirations and seismic levels of teen stress. Stanford University is three miles from my house. The parents of the students I work with—many of them immigrants, all of them with extravagant ambitions—want their children to end up there so badly you can feel their need across the room. Or, you know, maybe not Stanford. Maybe Princeton. Or Yale. Certainly not a public school, unless it's Berkeley or UCLA.[1]

I don't judge them. After all, who am I to judge? My parents brought me to the United States from the former Soviet Union when I was nine in pursuit of the usual gilded promises immigrants chase: freedom, economic opportunity, a better life for their children. I was supposed to go to Stanford and become an engineer (I did neither). Instead, I majored in English, got married, went to graduate school, had a baby, and got a PhD in comparative literature. Then my son was diagnosed with autism, and my husband and I pushed him through years of intensive behavioral therapy, and then I had two more children, which seemed like a good idea at the time, and I began working in the Office of Undergraduate Admission at Stanford, which also seemed like a good idea at the time. Then I became an independent college counselor to some of the most tightly wound students and families in the world while my own children unraveled. I've been living at the intersection of unbridled ambition and

1. For this I vigorously blame the *U.S. News & World Report*, which first published "America's Best Colleges" in 1983. It's not like people didn't know that Harvard or Yale or Princeton or Stanford were good schools before 1983, it's just that it does something to a person psychologically to know that School X is the "best" (i.e., in the top ten in the country) and School Y is only fifty-seventh. In reality, the top ten colleges and universities in the United States (according to the *U.S. News & World Report*, anyway), represent 0.03 percent of all four-year colleges and universities in the country. If prohibitively high selectivity is the only criterion of excellence, there are about twenty-three schools in the United States that have admit rates below 10 percent. They include, in addition to the usual suspects, the College of the Ozarks and the Curtis School of Music. But those, of course, are not the schools whose siren songs lure students and parents to their doom.

family dysfunction for two decades now, and you learn a thing or two living there—including that there are parents who will stop at nothing to do what they think is best for their children. Myself included.

To conceive a child is to enter into a state of expectancy; to raise a child is to entertain an endless succession of expectations, major and minor, thwarted and fulfilled. This is a book about lofty expectations—my parents' for me, mine for my own children, my students' parents for *their* children—and about the consequences of those expectations. Because I vicariously apply to college dozens of times every fall (which puts me in a weird, suspended state of perpetual adolescence), I've structured this book as a series of responses to college essay prompts. Many of these prompts ask broad, sweeping questions about community, family, success, aspirations, and, yes, obstacles and failures. For fifteen years, I've encouraged and coaxed and occasionally dragged my students through the essay-writing process, asking them to mine the minutiae of their own experiences, to be specific and honest and self-aware—all while pushing my own demons out of sight. And all along, the question has pulsed in the back of my mind: How would I, knowing what I know now, answer these prompts if they were directed to me?

Here are my responses. I did not adhere to the specified word count[2] because I'm an adult and I can do whatever I want.[3]

---

2. For those unfamiliar with college essays, the word counts range from 50 to 800 words. The personal statement in the Common Application has a maximum word count of 650 words. I find MIT's invitation to students to describe the world they come from and how it has shaped their dreams and aspirations in 250 words or fewer particularly cruel, but Stanford's 50-word "What is the greatest problem faced by society today?" isn't far behind.

3. Within reason, obviously. I'm not a sociopath.

PART ONE
POSSIBILITIES

▶ Describe the world you come from; for example, your family, clubs, school, community, city, or town. How has that world shaped your dreams and aspirations?

—MIT

Palo Alto can be beguiling: the palm trees, the exquisite gardens with chromatic waves of tulips, hydrangeas, and roses, the extravagant explosions of bougainvillea, the voluptuous breeze on a sun-bright day, the banks of fog rolling over the Santa Cruz Mountains that separate us from the beach to which we hardly ever go because the traffic is horrible. At the western edge is the Town and Country Shopping Center, landscaped with native shrubs and rugged, earth-colored stonework meant to resemble a hacienda that in this case also boasts a Bar Method studio and an Athleta, plus micro-batch ice cream in flavors like Earl Gray Lavender and TCHO Chocolate. There's also Vietnamese street food, plus designer tacos, plus a beauty spa founded by a Russian immigrant where the Asian women who do the manicures and pedicures and facials wear name tags with names the white clients can pronounce: Tiffany, Jenny, Lisa. It's a town both charmed and haunted, kissed by abundance, built on a bedrock of barely contained dread.

The story of Palo Alto is inextricably intertwined with the story of Stanford University, which begins in 1884 with a dead child. Leland Stanford Jr. was born to Jane Lathrop Stanford and Leland Stanford after eighteen childless years and, in a particularly awful bit of irony, died of typhoid on a grand tour of Europe that was the nineteenth-century equivalent of today's junior-year college tour—a trip that would have inaugurated the next promising chapter of his life. He was just shy of his sixteenth birthday. His shattered parents declared that the children of California would be their children and, less than a year after his death, founded a university to honor his memory.

The Stanford campus, all 8,180 tawny, sprawling acres of it, is surrounded by Palo Alto, a city built, like Stanford, on the twin pillars of education and grief. Palo Alto High School—or Paly, as everyone calls it—is just east of Stanford and just west of the railroad tracks, which run right behind the school. But the suicides by train—so many they've been called an epidemic—have been largely by students who go to Gunn, Paly's crosstown rival. Which is not to say that Paly students are not perpetually stressed, that they don't abuse Adderall, that they don't cut themselves, that they don't drink to excess, that they don't have eating disorders, anxiety disorders, OCD, depression, insomnia. They are and they do, and so do the girls in pleated blue skirts who go to Castilleja, a private all-girls' school located in a handsome shingled Craftsman-style building a stone's throw from Paly. For the record, we don't throw stones in Palo Alto; instead, we engage in vitriolic exchanges on Nextdoor and in the online comments section of the *Palo Alto Weekly*, criticizing other people's parenting, which is evidently to blame for everything from careless bicyclists to teen depression and anxiety, and complaining about everything from rude drivers to the size of the Halloween crowds at Steve Jobs's house, where full-sized candy bars are routinely distributed to legions of trick-or-treaters and their gawking parents. A group of Palo Alto parents is currently suing the Palo Alto Unified School District for unfair math class placement practices that the plaintiffs claim hinder students' ability to attend highly selective colleges. In Palo Alto, grief and grievance are two sides of the same stone.

A hundred and thirty-five years after its founding, Stanford is all anyone in Palo Alto can talk about. It fills the dreams of hundreds of thousands of high school students and exercises an invisible gravitational pull, like those tractor beams in *Star Wars*. It was founded to be inclusive, to be embracing, to commemorate a child lost too young, to pay tribute to his love of learning, his curiosity, his joy. It was coeducational at a time when universities were typically single-sex, nondenominational when most universities were religious, practical when most were abstruse. Now it admits roughly 2,000 applicants every year and roughly rejects 45,000, some of whom—and I don't mean to understate the horror of it—throw themselves under trains. It compels parents to do ridiculous things: make donations in the millions, photoshop their landlocked children to look like Olympic-bound sailors, move to Palo Alto from all over the world to pay several million dollars for crappy fixer-upper houses with plywood walls and single-pane windows that fog up in the winter so they can send their kids to the local public schools ("Award-winning PA schools," the real estate ads say), or, in some cases, to one of the local private schools—Castilleja, Harker, Nueva, Menlo, Crystal Springs, Sacred Heart, Woodside Priory. Schools with a carefully pre-screened, pre-tested, pre-approved student body, schools in mansions built by California robber barons, schools that cost over $50,000 a year. Then they come see me for college counseling.

Yep: me. Irena Smith, née Irina Averbukh, who arrived in the United States from the Soviet Union with her parents in 1978, speaking approximately seventeen words of English (ten of them numbers); who graduated with a 3.3 GPA from the same suburban Silicon Valley high school as Steve Jobs and Steve Wozniak; who only got into the UCLA by the grace of some benevolent and distracted god; who wore heavy black eyeliner and smoked Benson & Hedges menthol Ultra Lights and cut class and eschewed capital letters throughout her teens and spent her college years aspiring to but never quite achieving the bohemian nonchalance of a sleek, dark-haired gamine in a Parisian garret (while in actuality living in a 1960s walk-up apartment in Westwood Village and sporting permed hair and slouchy socks and off-the-shoulder oversized sweatshirts in slavish imitation of Jennifer Beals in *Flashdance*). Today those delusions of grandeur include offering trenchant responses via languid contralto to Terry Gross on an imagined appearance on *Fresh Air* and fantasizing about becoming Alexis Rose on *Schitt's Creek*, even though I'm neither the right age nor the right build, nor do I possess Alexis's sartorial audacity. But yes, that's me: playing Words with Friends on my phone, attending Monday night improv classes, leaving the three books I'm reading simultaneously on the kitchen counter, marching in place while brushing my teeth so I can hit my daily Fitbit step goal, shopping for organic salad mix at Trader Joe's, and taking a fish oil capsule every morning, just in case. I'm also the one wondering at least a few times every week how I suddenly got so old and how the hell I ended up where I am, who I am, doing what I do.

This is not, of course, why high school students and their parents come to see me. They come to see me because I have a PhD, because I taught at UCLA and Stanford, because I spent four years reading applications in Stanford's Office of Undergraduate Admission.[4] The parents who come to see

4. "Admission" is singular, because yes, it *is* that hard to get in.

me want their children to be happy and successful, and the only way to make their children happy and successful is to make sure they get into one of the HYPS schools. (Yes, there is, indeed, an acronym for Harvard, Yale, Princeton, and Stanford. Perhaps because uttering those full names aloud would violate superstition or take up too much valuable time. Or perhaps because it would force an acknowledgement of the subtext, "Nothing but the best will do for my extraordinarily special child—or, by extension, for me.") They come to see me because I'm meant to be the Virgil in Dante's *Inferno*, guiding them through the ten circles of application hell, or else a friendly animal sidekick in a Disney movie—Jiminy Cricket, say—or a combination of Sam Gamgee and Gandalf in *The Lord of the Rings*. Steady, reliable, wise.

They come to me with complaints, demands, questions, and conjectures. Here's a very partial list, in no particular order:

- My child has no spark.
- My child has an 88.7 in math/chemistry/English that the teacher wouldn't round up to an A-.
- My child spends too much time doing one activity (often, this is an unconventional, genuinely compelling pursuit like board game design or performing magic tricks or sewing or songwriting that the kid would do even if no one were looking and will likely help their application far more than a summer internship or a pay-to-play summer enrichment program).
- It's so hard to get into college ("college" is usually a signifier for HYPS and not Case Western or UC Merced).
- The schools are brutally competitive. "I don't want Blake's description of his school to sound like a fight to the death in District 12," a mom said to me once,

"because it's not really like that. Well, it sort of is, but he shouldn't put that in his essay, right?"
- My child is Indian.
- My child is Asian.
- My child won't work on his essay (which is abysmal) but he also wants to visit his girlfriend in Maryland and he has sports practice so how can he write a compelling essay without doing any of the work? Also, the deadline is in four days.
- My child studies too much and is horribly stressed.
- My child doesn't study enough and spends too much time playing video games.
- My friend's child's college essay is funny. Should my (deadly serious) child's be too?
- I read on the internet that [insert a particularly outlandish or unsubstantiated morsel about college applications here]. Please parse it for me.

My work is a combination of cheerleader, strategic planner, family therapist, and writing coach. My current hourly rate is $500/hour, which people pay without blinking and which makes me feel alternately like a big deal and a total fraud. Yes, I really am that good at finding a student's spark, at helping them find their voice, at facilitating the translation of messy lived experience into a five-page application, but a lot of my work also involves common sense. A lot of it is suffused by my experience as a former child and a current parent and an ability to see that while this process is shockingly new to the families I work with, it is at the same time terribly old. It is a rite of passage, albeit one that's been corrupted by colleges' marketing departments, the internet, the *U.S. News & World Report* rankings, and yes, people like me.

I never set out to be a college counselor. What I really am qualified to do, if you must know, is talk a lot (it's a point of pride to this day that I was voted Most Likely to Talk to Anyone or Anything about Anyone or Anything as a senior at Homestead High School in Cupertino) and tell long-winded stories and drink coffee and gesticulate expansively. That was the whole point of graduate school, which was a place where you could hold forth about books to other graduate students or to a captive audience of undergrads and cradle Styrofoam cups of coffee while smoking on the terrace on the third floor of Royce Hall, back in the halcyon days when you could still smoke without people looking at you like you were a serial killer. I expected to spend my life happily ensconced in my ivory tower, gossiping about fellow graduate students and trafficking in stories, celebrating the pliability of language, the infinite variety of human experience, from the sublime to the ridiculous to the tragic. To be clear, trafficking in *other* people's stories from a safe distance. That was the plan, anyway. But here's the funny thing about stories and about expectations for that matter: they never turn out quite the way you think they will.

When people ask me what it's like to live in Palo Alto—what it's like to be a *college admissions counselor* in Palo Alto, where 13 percent of the population holds advanced degrees, where the median income is well over six figures a year and the median home value is over $3 million, where everyone has to be, and to have, top-ranked everything—I am sometimes tempted to quote Quentin Compson in *Absalom, Absalom!* "I don't hate it," I want to say, "I don't hate it. I don't. I don't." The truth is, I don't hate it—really, I don't—but the echoes between the Greek tragedies referenced in Faulkner's novel and my own life are uncanny. Misguided parents, outsized expectations, scarred children, relentless striving, a house doomed to devour itself, people blind to the seeds of destruction they themselves have sown, and terrible consequences to actions taken with the best of intentions. And that's just at my own house.

▶ Everyone belongs to many different communities and/or groups defined by (among other things) shared geography, religion, ethnicity, income, cuisine, interest, race, ideology, or intellectual heritage. Choose one of the communities to which you belong, and describe that community and your place within it.

—UNIVERSITY OF MICHIGAN

My husband David and I moved to Palo Alto in 1999 because it was safe and green and had good schools and my father's telecommunications company, which he had founded with his brother Boris in the early '90s, had gone public the year before. My parents gifted us enough stock to make a down payment on what seemed at the time to be an egregiously overpriced fixer-upper three-bedroom house with crappy plywood walls and single-pane windows that fogged up in the winter.

In 1999, Palo Alto was where ambitious, hard-working people, or the descendants of ambitious, hard-working people, or people who were lucky enough to be in the right place at the right time, ended up. Three years prior, I had completed my dissertation on displacement and semantic instability in the novels of Henry James and Vladimir Nabokov and almost immediately got a job teaching an undergraduate humanities course at Stanford. David was doing a National Institute of

Mental Health fellowship in psychopharmacology, also at Stanford. We had been married for nine years; before that, we had conducted a four-year long-distance relationship, primarily by letter and occasionally phone, while David was at Cornell and I was at UCLA. The relationship culminated in a lavish wedding at the Fairmont Hotel in San Francisco, which my parents, whose own wedding ceremony entailed standing in a long line of other couples at the Moscow Marriage Palace to get their passports stamped, had taken out a second mortgage to pay for. We arrived in Palo Alto full of hubris, which seemed fitting given that we were moving into a city practically exploding with it. The year before we bought our house, two Stanford graduate students—one of them a son of Russian Jewish immigrants who arrived in the United States at roughly the same time as my parents—began work on a search engine whose name would soon become a ubiquitous verb, and Pierre Omidyar and Jeffrey Skoll became instant billionaires[5] after eBay went public. The year after we bought our house, PayPal cleared the one million user mark. People around us were practically minting money. The air was heady with promise and possibility and jacaranda blooms. What could possibly go wrong? (Okay, there *was* a weird thing that happened on our first night in the new house: a freak electrical storm that came out of nowhere in the middle of the night. No rain—just ten minutes of violent dry wind that shook the house and thunder that rattled the windows and unbearably bright flashes of apocalyptic, white-blue lightning. And then it was over, just as suddenly as it began—such an egregiously, screamingly obvious ill omen that I shoved it down and decided to never think about it again. I mean, even if it was a warning, what would we do?)[6]

---

5. My spellcheck thinks "billionaires" is wrong and wants me to replace it with "millionaires." Clearly, my spellcheck doesn't realize that in Palo Alto, there's no such thing as hyperbole.
6. "You already know what you're going to do," says Fleabag's therapist. "Everybody does."

▶ Briefly elaborate on one of your extracurricular activities, a job you hold, or responsibilities you have for your family.

—STANFORD UNIVERSITY[7]

Twenty years before David and I moved to Palo Alto, in fall of 1978, I learned everything there was to know about promise and possibility from American television. That winter, my parents and I arrived in San Francisco as

7. Every week or two, I get a query from a parent of a sixth or seventh grader about wanting to know all the right things they should be doing to maximize their child's chances of getting into a highly selective college. Literally, "all the right things." Sometimes the email mentions "strategic planning" or "positioning" or "packaging." Once, the query came from a parent of a six-year-old with a "strong interest in Stanford." Another indicated that her son was "passionate" about attending an Ivy League school. Because these schools are highly selective, one parent went on to say, we'd like to get an early start on planning. The email ended with a smiley face.

I have a text expander shortcut for such situations. I type "tooearly," and here's what populates: "Thank you for your message and your interest. I don't engage with students younger than ninth grade, partly because I have no expertise in working with a population that young, but predominantly because I believe strongly that college counseling of any kind should begin no earlier than high school. Prior to that, it's simply too early to begin a conversation about aspects of a process still many years in the future with a student who is still growing and developing in so many ways; for now, I would suggest letting your child enjoy doing what they love—both in and out of the classroom."

What I really wish the text expander would do was say "Leave your poor kid alone or so help me god, I'll call Child Protective Services." Or, if it were a really expansive text expander, I would tell them this story. Not because it ends with ". . . and I turned out okay" (the jury is still out on that), but because you can learn a lot from wasting your time after school. I certainly did.

Soviet refugees after a blissful (to me, anyway), five-month interlude—two weeks in Vienna and four-plus months in Rome during which I did not go to school, learned Italian from the noisy, exuberant kids who played in the courtyard of our apartment building, and read haphazardly from books in the Russian-language lending library. And then the bliss ended.

We moved into an apartment on a noisy corner of 23rd Avenue and Geary Boulevard, upstairs from Yu's House of Teriyaki, whose purple and red neon sign blinked through the window of the living room where I slept on a mattress on the floor. I had been placed, on full scholarship, into a conservative Jewish day school by Jewish Family and Children's Services; the school was in tony Pacific Heights; I had two outfits to my name, a bad haircut, and, by then, a primitive command of English. I spent most of the year avoiding my classmates, who, like the nine-year-old sharks that they were, smelled blood in the water (or perhaps the cold chicken wrapped in tinfoil I brought for lunch in a plastic grocery bag) and moved in for the kill. I came home every day and sobbed on my mattress while my parents tried clumsily to console me, promising that one day I would speak English so well that I would correct *their* grammar mistakes. "That will *never* happen!" I would yell, and then cry some more, my back to the darkening window, while "Teriyaki. Teriyaki. Teriyaki" blinked on and off in muted purple and pink on the facing wall.

We learned a lot that year. We learned that when a store clerk says Sears is just fifteen minutes down Geary, he means by car, not on foot. We learned to break open a fortune cookie before eating it. My parents bought a used 1973 Plymouth Satellite and found jobs in Silicon Valley. With their new salaries, they rented an apartment on a quieter street and bought a couch and a colored television. They enrolled me in Alamo Elementary School, a nearby public school full of children from all over the world who also did not speak English. And I began to discover America.

1949 Clement was the first place to which I had my own key, knotted on an increasingly grubby string around my neck. And at Alamo Elementary, which was a live-and-let-live kind of place, I learned all kinds of things, like states and capitals, the Pledge of Allegiance, and that cold chicken could be traded for pork buns or rice paper rolls at lunch.

My parents were gone from 7:00 a.m. to 6:00 p.m. I was entrusted with getting to and from school, keeping the apartment reasonably tidy, doing my homework, and, on Tuesdays and Thursdays, walking myself to my nearby gymnastics class. But on Monday, Wednesday, and Friday afternoons I was free. And that was when I discovered after-school television.

My world exploded into a multicolored phantasmagoria: Star Wars action figures, My Pretty Pony, dolls who drank water and wet their diaper, and cereal. A lot of cereal. I was invited to go cuckoo for Cocoa Puffs, to follow the Lucky Charms leprechaun to the end of the rainbow, and to laugh at the silly Trix rabbit. But it was the sunny yellow box of Corn Pops that captured my heart and my taste buds.

Every Monday, Wednesday, and Friday after school, I poured a heaping bowl of Corn Pops, covered them with banana slices, and liberally glugged milk on top before plopping in front of the TV. Who even needed the other stuff—the orange juice, the diagonally sliced toast—that the commercials insisted was part of this complete breakfast? I had it all: cereal, TV, and parents not due home for three or more hours, depending on traffic.

I usually managed to catch the tail end of *The Tom and Jerry Show* on Channel 2 before switching to Channel 44 for *The Brady Bunch*, an instant favorite. I quickly developed a crush on Peter, who bore an uncanny resemblance to my real-life fifth-grade crush, Daniel Kenneth. To be honest, I had a crush on the entire Brady family: on Alice, with her corny jokes and inexhaustible supply of cookies; on the Brady girls (okay, not Jan); on their pink ruffled room; on their mom, who had such kind eyes and who sewed costumes from scratch. And they ate such interesting food! What, exactly, were pork chops and applesauce? What was a barbeque? Why was Alice so concerned about slamming doors when she made a soufflé? And speaking of Alice, how did one get a maid in a nifty blue uniform who would hand you a lunch bag every morning and pick up your stuff?

My parents, meanwhile, had entirely different ideas about what constituted the most productive use of my time, and one day, my father summarily decreed that I was no longer allowed to watch TV after school. So I nodded earnestly and promised to make better use of my time. The next afternoon, I made sure to turn off the TV *before* my parents returned. But my father was no dummy, and one day, when I walked into the living room with my cereal bowl and turned the switch to "on," the TV screen remained dark and cold.

It had not been a good week. At school, a girl with whom I had forged a tentative friendship publicly accused me of liking Daniel Kenneth. My Russian gymnastics coach said I hung off the high bar with all the grace of a sausage—"*kak sosiska*" were his exact words. And there was something else: several weeks earlier, I had spotted a mind-boggling offer on my most recent box of Corn Pops. Three proof-of-purchase seals and $1.50 for shipping and handling would get you an inflatable beach ball with "Kellogg's Corn Pops" emblazoned on a sunny yellow background. I'd already wheedled the money from my parents and dropped the envelope in a mailbox and now was breathlessly checking the mail in our small entry every day to find nothing. Nothing! I could almost hear the shysters at Kellogg's cackling maliciously somewhere in Battle Creek, Michigan.

It was in this dark state that I tackled the problem of the television. I had never been technologically minded, and as I nudged the set sideways to investigate the tangle of wires in the back, a small part of me hoped I would be electrocuted, which would serve my parents right for taking away the thing I loved most in the world. But I managed to turn the TV back on without incident, catching the last half of *The Brady Bunch* and my new favorite—*Gilligan's Island*. I loved the lush tropical setting, the Professor's crisp white shirts, the flirtatious mole above Ginger's pouty lips, and the way Gilligan and the Skipper bickered even though it was clear they were friends for life. I loved how you could construct an entire civilization from bamboo poles and coconut shells. I loved it so much that I barely remembered to unplug the TV before my parents came home and was slightly out of breath as I slid behind my desk and opened my math textbook.

Disaster was only temporarily averted. One afternoon, returning from work a little earlier than usual, my dad casually placed his hand on top of the TV and gave me a long look. "Hmm," he said. "Can you tell me why the TV is warm?"

My parents called me a liar and a sneak. They said they couldn't trust me again. They couldn't believe I would choose to sit like a ruminant in front of the television instead of working hard and learning. *Kak korova* (like a cow), they said.

I listened while my resentment swelled. I did not want to work hard and learn. I wanted to be left alone in my little oasis, awash in a sea of cold milk dotted with pale yellow archipelagos of sliced bananas. I wanted to listen endlessly to Mr. and Mrs. Howell round their vowels and to see the smirk on Cindy's face as she stumbled onto Bobby kissing Millicent. I wanted to be the invisible ninth person at the

Brady dinner table, the eighth castaway on Gilligan's Island. I wouldn't watch any more TV, I promised. I would apply myself! But those were lies and in all likelihood my parents knew it, too.

It occurs to me now that my parents had good reason to be upset. They left everything and everyone they knew so that we could have a better life in this new country. No one in my family had heard of Horatio Alger, but we didn't need to; it was clear that in America, hungry huddled masses yearning to breathe free could, by dint of hard work, become wealthy and successful. And here was their only child, who, at barely nine, had read *Anna Karenina* and Bulgakov's *The Master and Margarita* en route to the United States, who kept an illustrated journal of our travels, spending every afternoon seated in front of a braying television set and consuming fluorescent yellow pellets by the bucketful.

An uneasy peace settled over our family after that. I watched a measly half hour of TV before sitting down to do my homework. The year was drawing to a close, and the windows were pitch-black by the time my parents came home. Everything, it felt, was waning. And then, one overcast afternoon, I came home from school, stuck my hand hopelessly in the mailbox, and there it was: a brown mailer with my name on it. Inside was a deflated yellow beach ball that smelled intoxicatingly of plastic and cheap ink and kept promises. I perched on the bottom step and blew into the plastic mouthpiece with all my might. Fully inflated, the ball looked exactly like the beach ball on the box of Corn Pops—only this one was dazzlingly real, and it was mine, nestled cozily at my feet while I ate Corn Pops and watched Marcia and Greg squabble over who got to sleep in the attic.

Who was to say which version of the American dream was more valid, or more true? While my parents were at work pursuing their version of it, I was at home pursuing mine, the taste of Corn Pops and plastic mixing on my lips. Yes, America was the place where hard work and perseverance might win the day, but it was also the land of plenty—the land where plenty begat more plenty, where you were rewarded for wanting and consuming what you loved best, where if you ate Corn Pops faithfully and then waited patiently, good things would come to you. Good things would come.

▶ List the titles of the books, essays, poetry, short stories or plays you read outside of academic courses that you enjoyed most during secondary/high school.

—COLUMBIA UNIVERSITY[8]

In one of my earliest memories, my father is reading me Pushkin's "The Tale of Tsar Saltan" on the scratchy red-and-black flecked couch in our Moscow apartment, and I look up at him in amazement when I recognize that the refrain about the ship dancing over the waves repeats between each segment of the story and he smiles back to

8. When I meet with students for the first time, I make a point of finding out what they like to read, and if they don't read, I harp on them to start reading. This is because reading helps with English papers, with history papers, with class participation, with the verbal skills section of the SAT, with college essays, and with having an answer ready when they're asked on college applications what their favorite books, newspapers, magazines, or blogs are. Reading also helps with what Stanford Office of Admission, rather pretentiously, calls intellectual vitality—an elusive quality that basically means the student is more than the sum of their grades and test scores, that they cherish learning for its own sake, that they're deeply curious. Reading books—for which I have an almost mystical reverence—is a pretty reliable indication of intellectual vitality. I've geeked out with students over Nathan Hill's *The Nix*, Helene Wecker's *The Golem and the Jinni*, Nella Larsen's *Passing*, Giles Milton's *Ministry of Ungentlemanly Warfare*, Isabelle Wilkerson's *The Warmth of Other Suns*, Mira Jacob's *Good Talk*, and, more than once, Bulgakov's *The Master and Margarita*. I've never forgotten the story an English professor told our seminar about Henry James conferences, where Jamesians will approach one another and breathlessly say "Chapter 42!"—a cryptic statement if ever there was one, except for James devotees, who will immediately recognize the reference to Isabel Archer's fireside vigil in *The Portrait of a Lady* and light up like a Christmas tree.

acknowledge that, yes, it's a pretty neat trick. My parents owned Boris Pasternak translations of all of Shakespeare's plays and Samuil Marshak's translations of Burns and Blake, and I read most of them before we left Moscow. Like most Soviet school children, I was made to memorize patriotic ditties at school, but at home, my parents encouraged me to memorize Pushkin poems and recite them to guests at dinner parties. And then our beautiful Russian tongue was gone, replaced by an incomprehensible babble of English.

My father spoke passable English when we arrived, but my mother knew maybe ten words, and spent the first several weeks in America mutely terrified, fleeing from the room and seeking refuge in a corner of the kitchen if our phone rang because my father wanted her to answer it to practice her English, an idea she found about as appealing as a root canal. When she did answer the phone, she couldn't understand anything the caller was saying, and if the caller was a mother from my fourth-grade class who was trying to let her know the make and color of the carpool car that would be coming to get me the following morning, she would yell loudly and cheerfully into the receiver, "Yes! Yes! Tenk you!" and hang up, and then tearfully confess that she understood nothing—not what kind of car would come get me, not what time I could expect to be picked up, not a single shred of useful information except possibly for the word "carpool." The next morning, she would hustle me out of bed at 6:30 a.m. so we could stand at the corner of 23rd Avenue and Geary at 7:00 a.m. (which she figured was early enough for me not to miss my ride because whenever it was coming it couldn't possibly be before seven) and scan passing cars until one would slow down, and if there were children roughly my age in the car and a friendly-looking woman at the wheel she would deposit me inside and hope fervently that I would come back safely at the end of the day. But by the time I was in seventh grade, she graduated to carrying on conversations with her colleagues at work and faithfully watching *Dynasty* every Wednesday at 9:00 p.m., and, thanks to my younger, more au courant Aunt Irina, she discovered the novels of Howard Fast, Jackie Collins, and Judith Krantz. And in those books, she discovered a whole substratum of the English language: swearing.

In the afterword to his own Russian translation of *Lolita*, Vladimir Nabokov blames the aesthetic shortcomings of the Russian version on the dissonant jangling of his "rusty Russian strings," but equally so, he blames the fact that in English, certain words and concepts are rendered better than in Russian. Better in Russian: nature and emotions (such as *toska*, the utterly untranslatable word encompassing longing, nostalgia, ennui, soul-pain—all of which my mother was quite possibly experiencing, but all of which, in my eighth-grade solipsism, were to me terra incognita). Better in English: automotive parts, sex (pretty much unspeakable in Russian), and swear words (ditto, unless uttered by drunken vulgarians). As a later-in-life learner of English uninhibited by social norms (at least not at home), my mother reveled shamelessly in American swearing.

My father winced when she read choice passages out loud. "Sveta," he would say, "as a non-native speaker, you can't really feel the temperature of the word. I recommend being more careful." I liked the idea that words could be blazing hot or bone-cold, or even lukewarm. Certainly *I* could feel the temperature of the words my mother called out from the kitchen table, or from her bedroom (she was in the habit of reading in bed), because the embarrassment of hearing them in her accented English would creep into my cheeks like a hot wave. "Listen to this, Irisha," she'd chortle, "This one guy is mad at his friend, so he says, 'I'll tell you where your brains are, you dumb prick: in your asshole!"

And then she would cackle triumphantly, and I would be left wondering if other eighth graders also had mothers who did this.

As it happened, the book that launched my mother's joyful wallow in profanity—Howard Fast's *The Immigrants*—was the first installment of a sweeping historical saga about the Lavettes, a French-Italian family that fled hunger and destitution in Sicily, and the Levys, who fled hunger and pogroms in Eastern Europe a few decades prior. At my mother's behest (and because, frankly, I was curious about what else was in the book other than swearing), I read it, too, and discovered an enchanting world: swearing, yes, but also history (The San Francisco earthquake! World War I! The Great Depression!), romance, and sex.

By today's standards, the sex was pretty tame, but to a fairly sheltered thirteen-year-old, it was entirely scandalous. Daniel Lavette, the book's protagonist, has a blonde ice goddess of a wife, whom he marries against her parents' wishes, and later, when that marriage fizzles, takes a Chinese mistress. He was clearly a man of enormous appetites, and I found myself alternately repelled and fascinated by his exploits, unable to keep myself from rereading the scene where Dan and Jean, the ice goddess, have sex for the first time in the waterfront shack from which he is building a shipping empire. (In retrospect, the sex was rapey and cringe-inducing, but I was too mesmerized by the thrusting and gasping to notice). *The Immigrants* was followed by the second installment in the series, *Second Generation* (more history, World War II this time, and more sex), and then by a long series of sequels that were not nearly as compelling either historically or sexually. By that point, I had started high school, and together, my mom and I discovered Jackie Collins' *Hollywood Wives* and Judith Krantz's *Scruples* and *Mistral's Daughter* and were firmly in soft-porn territory.

Dazzled as she was by the glamorous clothes and shocking plot twists and the opulent lifestyles of movie stars and fashion moguls, my mom seemed not to care that at age thirteen, I was reading material that by today's standards would be highly unsuitable for an eighth-grader.

The thing about my family is that we did not talk about sex—pretty much ever. When I was ten, my mom pinned me with a look of such consternation while telling me we were going for a walk around the block that I assumed I was about to get in major trouble. But no; a hundred or so yards from our front door, she said, "I'm about to tell you some very uncomfortable things, so please don't ask me any questions." Then she shared some clinical details about intercourse and suggested that I not engage in premarital sex before marriage. The explanation lasted long enough for us to go around the block: down Clement Street to 22nd Avenue, right on 22nd, right on Geary, right on 21st, right on Clement, back to our front door. I did not ask any questions, and by the time we reentered our apartment, we had clearly reached an unspoken agreement to never speak of sex again. When I was thirteen and started my period, I was told we didn't use tampons, only pads (because, also by unspoken implication, the only thing that went into one's vagina was one's husband's penis, on one's wedding night). It wasn't until I was a sophomore in college that a friend coached me through the mechanics of inserting a tampon while she was in the neighboring toilet stall, and my life has never been the same since.

In fairness, my mom grew up in Soviet Russia, where sex was on par with private enterprise: shameful, degenerate, not to be discussed, and to be engaged in only in times of necessity—so much so that her own mother failed to instruct her in even the most fundamental aspects of human biology. (At least I had *Are You There, God? It's Me, Margaret*, so unlike my mom I knew what a period was and waited for it with breathless anticipation until I got it the second time and realized what a crock of shit that book was.) Interestingly, after *I* turned thirteen, Grandma Ester, the same grandmother who had neglected to instruct my mom about menstruation, casually mentioned, apropos of nothing, that if I ever married someone non-Jewish, she would curse me until her grave, and then some. Roughly during the same time, my father's mother, proper and soft-spoken Grandma Tsilya, mentioned—also apropos of nothing, as I was watching her roll out dough for *varnishkes*—that all naked men were hideously ugly. So that was the sum of my sexual knowledge: no tampons, no premarital sex, no marrying non-Jews, and no questions. Also: ugly naked men.

My romantic prospects in high school were not particularly promising, which made the prohibition against premarital sex a non-issue. I led a reasonably chaste life. Which is not to say that I did not avidly seek out the sexy parts in pretty much every book I got my hands on, or that I did not read them over and over with a yearning curiosity. But this, too, was a non-issue until Shirley Conran's *Lace* came along and turned our world on its axis.

In winter of my junior year, previews started appearing on TV: an ornate hotel room, four handsome older women, one voluptuous younger woman staring at them defiantly before uttering the immortal words: "Which one of you bitches is my mother?" There followed a montage of voracious kissing, operatic moaning, and gymnastic writhing set in sumptuous bedrooms across Europe and the United States. It looked stupid and over the top, but it also looked wildly tantalizing. Like, must-see TV tantalizing.

My mother—who wouldn't miss an episode of *Dynasty* to save her life, who chortled over words like "cocksucker" and "prick" and "shitfaced," and who read Judith Krantz and Jackie Collins right alongside me—arbitrarily decided that we would not be watching *Lace* on television. Or maybe her prohibition wasn't arbitrary; maybe it was because I, and not she, found the show. Or maybe it was because the main character calls her mother a "bitch." Whatever the reason, we only had one TV, and that was that. But the miniseries was based on a book, and while the number of TVs at our house may have been limited to one, the number of copies of *Lace* out in the world was practically limitless. You'd think my problem was solved, but here too she thwarted me. When she caught me thumbing through *Lace* at B. Dalton's at the mall, she told me to put it back on the shelf. "It's trash," she said, against my protest.

This was the first time my mother denied me a book. Before that moment, she encouraged omnivorous, audacious reading. She had never said I was too young or too ill-equipped to read anything; she had, in fact, mocked me for reading "children's books" when I came home with a school library copy of *The Witch of Blackbird Pond*. She had handed me Bulgakov's *The Master and Margarita* and *The Fatal Eggs* when I was nine (I was haunted by nightmares about vampires, demons, and gargantuan reptiles for several months after). She didn't seem to mind that *Anna Karenina* was a book about lust and adultery and betrayal and suicide by train or that Isaac Babel's *Red Cavalry* contained extravagantly violent scenes I can see in my mind's eye today. She was unbothered that the books of Leon Uris and Herman Wouk, which I inhaled throughout middle school and high school, contained Dantesque descriptions of mass murder, torture, and disfigurement. And speaking of Dante: we had a Russian translation of *The Inferno*—illustrated, even—in our home library, and she didn't mind that I read that either. Practically as a toddler!

The woman who had offered me nothing but open books was suddenly and utterly unreadable, and her cryptic obstinacy made me want *Lace* that much more. I was entitled to *Lace*. I needed *Lace*. I yearned for it. So I returned to B. Dalton alone several days later and purchased my very own copy with my babysitting money.

When Walt Whitman wrote that "the secret of it all, is to write in the gush, the throb, the flood, of the moment," he may very well have been anticipating the breathless, propulsive rhythms of Shirley Conran's novel. *Lace* contained multitudes—gushing and throbbing and pulsing and aching and flooding, plus a goldfish deployed in ways I never imagined a goldfish could be deployed, plus a convoluted mystery involving four women, a virile ruler of a fictional Middle Eastern kingdom, an adult film star, and possible incest. But above all, it offered the thrill of reading a book I wasn't supposed to be reading—until one day my mother stormed into my room to berate me for living in a pigsty (*kak svin'ya*—like a pig—she said), pointed out that the closet, not the floor, was where normal people kept their clothes, and flung open my closet door to emphasize her point. And there was *Lace*, splayed wantonly on a bed of thrift-store skirts and balled-up leg warmers and underwear.

I had disappointed my parents before (see: being caught in proximity of a warm television) and would go on to do so in the future, but never had I seen my mother so angry. Red-faced and shaking, she yelled that I was a liar, that I had gone behind her back, that I was reading filth and living in filth and that she couldn't stand the sight of me. As a coup de graçe, she ordered me out of the house, right now, this minute. I had had a driver's license for several months, and I grabbed my keys and stormed out. But then, as I drove away and the heady rush of adrenaline wore off, it occurred to me that I had nowhere to go. I did not have a close enough friend at whose house I could just show up. I couldn't see myself going to a restaurant, and I didn't want to drive around aimlessly and run out of gas. So

I went to the only place an awkward, self-conscious girl who had just gotten into a big fight with her mother would go: the Sunnyvale Public Library.

I found an empty desk and grabbed a book off a nearby shelf, which turned out to be a collection of American folk songs. And I sat there for at least an hour, staring through burning eyes at the lyrics to "Oh, Susannah!" (Don't you cry for me, indeed.) Going back to the house was unthinkable: I felt bitterly wounded by my mother's words—home was sacrosanct, and to tell one's only child to get the hell out was a mortal blow. Layered on top of the hurt was bewilderment (why was it okay to read *Hollywood Wives* but not *Lace*?), and on top of that was a seething resentment. Who did she think she was, this woman who yelled bad words in accented English, to police what I read? Who was she to exile me?

My predicament left me with few choices—sleep in the car, ask our neighbors with five kids if they had room for one more, or sit there miserably until the library closed, at which point I would be forced to decide what to do. I chose option three, and just before closing, right as the hopelessness and desperation crescendoed, my father appeared out of nowhere and asked if he could sit down.

I still have no idea how he found me, but seeing him dislodged whatever barrier was keeping the tears at bay and I swiped at my eyes and nodded in relief, chin trembling. He sat quietly for a while. I didn't trust myself to speak, so I said nothing. After a few minutes, he asked, "Where were you going to go when the library closed?"

I shrugged.

"You know that we were worried about you, right?"

I shrugged again.

The librarian announced on the PA system that the library was closing in five minutes and asked all patrons to bring their materials to the check-out desk.

"Let's go home," my dad said.

I shook my head fiercely.

"Irisha. Let's go home."

This time I found my voice. "She told me to get out. She said she didn't want to see my face anymore. I'm not going home."

"The library is now closing," said the librarian over the PA system. "All patrons are asked to leave at this time."

So we went to a nearby Jack in the Box on El Camino Real and shared an order of French fries while my dad brokered an agreement. I would come back home and apologize for sneaking the book into the house against my mom's express wishes. My dad let it be known that even if my mom never actually said so, she regretted losing her temper and telling me to get out. His own opinion—and he managed to say this without explicitly condemning what my mother had said, which I wanted him to do so badly my teeth hurt—was that we all belonged at home and that's all there was to it. We got into our separate cars, and my dad followed me back to our house.

Behind the half-open door to their dimly lit bedroom, I heard my mother ask my father "*Nashyol*?" ("Did you find her?"). She sounded congested, like she had been crying; *Good*, I thought, with a pang of grim satisfaction. Then my father beckoned me in, and my mom and I apologized clumsily to each other, and I slept in my own bed, not in the car, and many years later, when I asked her what it was about *Lace* that set her off, she told me she couldn't for the life of her remember.

What she did remember, vividly, was that yelling at me to leave the house was her worst moment as a parent. She also remembered her abject panic: I was a junior in high school and seemed utterly indifferent to my future. In fairness, it's not that I was indifferent to that future, it was just that it wasn't nearly as urgent to me as the heaving and thrusting and quivering I found in the pages of *Lace*. That fall, my father had purchased a fat SAT prep book and left it pointedly on my desk, but I ignored it. In my physics class, I passed flirtatious notes with two of the boys sitting near me instead of paying attention to lab instructions for our electricity unit and proceeded to blow the fuse in the classroom. I hid cigarettes in my LeSportsac purse and forbidden books in my closet. I was, in my mother's mind, on the road to perdition.

In *Jane Eyre,* Edward Rochester unburdens himself to Jane, assailing his first wife's pygmy intellect and giant propensities and calling her a woman at once intemperate and unchaste. I suspect no small part of my mother's panic was due to her own conflation of sex and stupidity; clearly, a daughter who evinced more interest in soft porn than SAT prep was going nowhere good. But that was what bound us, too—our shared affection for the vulgar and the overheated and the intemperate and the overblown, an affection that caused my father to shake his head and leave the room every Wednesday night as my mother and I settled down for the newest episode of *Dynasty*.[9]

Unlike my mother and me, my father had little use for high drama. He was born in 1941, four years before my mother and two months before Nazi Germany invaded the Soviet Union. My grandmother was evacuated from Odessa with my six-month-old father in her arms; when she was in the hospital giving birth, a nurse in the maternity ward muttered that the ward was full of baby boys, which was a clear portent of imminent war. I don't know whether it was a dark fatalism or something else that compelled her to name my father Marcus, after the Roman god of war. All I know is that in the winter of 1985, my soft-spoken, temperate father managed to weave between my mother and me a delicate peace.

9. She now watches *Real Housewives* because of course she does. I do not because a line has to be drawn somewhere.

▶ Most students choose their intended major or area of study based on a passion or inspiration that's developed over time. What passion or inspiration led you to choose this area of study?

—CARNEGIE MELLON UNIVERSITY[10]

In Rome in the fall of 1977, shabbily dressed, anxious-looking Russian-speaking people seemed to be everywhere: Soviet Jews caught, like us, in limbo. When we weren't squeezed four families at a time into four-bedroom, one-bathroom apartments and overflowing residential hotels or crammed by the dozens into decrepit villas in the nearby suburbs of Ostia and Ladispoli, we were waiting in the smoke-filled lobby of the Hebrew Immigrant Aid Society in Rome for harried case-workers to call us into an office where we would be appraised of our progress (or lack thereof) toward political asylum that would get us admitted to the United States, or Australia, or

10. On some days, it feels like every student I work with wants to major in computer science because that's where the money is. Parents complain that everyone wants to major in computer science, so it's impossible to get in—which is true, especially if a student is applying to colleges that have a single-digit admit rate—but they don't want to hear about other schools, or other majors, and they look to me to somehow square that circle. They don't care that Steve Jobs dropped out of Reed (where he studied Japanese calligraphy) or that Sergei Brin went to University of Maryland as an undergrad and then dropped out of his graduate program at Stanford or that Michael Dell never graduated from UT Austin or that Peter Thiel majored in philosophy.

Canada, or other destinations in Europe. We, all of us, were always waiting. And in the midst of all the waiting, my father taught me clever math tricks so that, for the last three months of 1977, I was a math genius.

I wish I could remember what, exactly, he taught me. All I know is that at age nine, I could multiply two- or three-digit numbers by other two- or three-digit numbers in my head in a couple of seconds, with devastating accuracy and without breaking a sweat.

It was a party trick that helped pass the time. Fellow émigrés waiting in the HIAS lobby or in the medical offices to have their blood tested for venereal diseases they might import into their new homeland would double-check my numbers on scraps of paper and shake their heads in awe, muttering, "*T'fyu, chyort*" ("bloody hell!"). I was the embodiment of the bright future awaiting all of us beyond the Atlantic, in America, where, if you had a head for numbers, as I clearly did, you could be wildly successful—you could work as an engineer, even. That was the dream.

Though my father held a master's degree in engineering, the space for "nationality" on his Soviet passport read "Jew"—and no one would hire a Jewish engineer. Instead, he worked makeshift jobs as a technician and a mechanic. My mother, similarly, had not been able to study philology in college: too many Jews. Chemistry, however, was under-enrolled, so she became a high school chemistry teacher without really wanting to.

My parents had many other reasons to emigrate, not least of which was my father's pronounced contrarian streak. The man couldn't stand being told what to do and had even less patience for being restricted in what he could read, think, and say, which made life under a totalitarian regime difficult. In his pocket, he carried a miniature notebook that held a Maksimilian Voloshin poem in his equally miniscule script, the one that begins with the lines: "To see all, all to understand, to take in every shape and color / To walk the world with burning feet . . ." In emigrating, he hoped to find a place where the qualities he held in esteem—imagination, curiosity, iconoclasticism—were prized rather than punished. And everyone knew that to get ahead in a meritocracy, you had to be smart.

It wasn't just about the math. For him, it was about literacy and competence—in everything. He taught me to read when I was three, giving me a split second to recognize a word (no sounding out syllables—that was for slow-witted dummies) and moving on to the next word over my indignant howls if I failed to recognize it. When I was seven, he made me memorize the multiplication table: "I should be able to wake you up in the middle of the night and ask you, 'What's seven times six?' and you should be able to answer without hesitation." He taught me about centrifugal force by spinning a glass of water in a circle in a mesh bag and made me commit Kipling's poem "If" to memory, both in its excellent Russian translation by Samuil Marshak (that was easy) and in the original English, which was no small feat because I spoke absolutely no English at the time. Same with "I have six honest serving men," an ode to insatiable curiosity that follows "The Elephant's Child" in *Just So Stories*, which also took about the same amount of time to memorize as standing in one of the ever-present Soviet-era lines: forever.

At school, that competence got me in trouble. All good Soviet first-graders were meant to march together in lock-step, as a collective, and here I was getting ahead of the collective—writing in cursive while everyone else was still printing or using a shortcut the teacher had not explained to solve an arithmetic problem or drawing a foreshortened street in accordance with the law of perspective my father had taught me. "*Ne bud' vyskochkoi*" (don't be a show-off, or, literally, "a jumper ahead"), my teacher would say. But my father wanted to jump ahead, and he wanted me to jump ahead, and secretly, I was pleased when my classmates clustered around me, tracing their fingers over my drawing in disbelief while they tried to understand the trick whereby a street on a two-dimensional piece of paper could look as though it were truly receding into the background in 3D.

My genius days ended when our asylum appeal was granted and we moved on to the United States. When I became a student at Brandeis Hillel Jewish Day School, I was prepared for ridicule over my English, and even, to some extent, over my clothes and mannerisms, but I was not prepared for the math. It was understood that it might take me a while to catch up as I learned the language, but math was universal. If anything, my unerring accuracy with paperless multiplication would put me ahead of everyone else. Math, after all, was unambiguous and unequivocal. It didn't care if you spoke English or Russian or had flowing feathered hair or a dorky Dorothy Hamill haircut.

But in America, it was the long division that got me. In the Russian system of notation, the divisor is to the right, not the left, of the dividend, and the lines that separate them are configured in a mirror image of the American arrangement. And even though flipping the two should have been easy, it proved to be my undoing.

When my father tried to explain—"You just reverse the dividend and the divisor, see?"—I balked. I could not, would not get my head around the fact that the numbers had to be reversed. The babble of English, with its odd idioms, was to be expected. But that math, the thing I was good at, the thing that elicited admiring whistles from adults, would betray me—that I could not bear.

My father tried multiple times, and multiple different ways, to explain to me that the problem was simply orthographic. But then it was 10:00 p.m., and at 11:30 p.m., he slapped the table in disgust and left the room and I put my head down and cried. Everything was backwards in this stupid country, even the math. My mother, who had been quietly commiserating from the hallway, took over. She patted my head, called me *Irishen'ka*, and tried to explain that the operation was exactly the same as the one I had done in Moscow. By 2:00 a.m., it was both of us crying at the kitchen table. "Tomorrow morning," my mother repeated the Russian saying, "will be wiser than the evening." But it never was.

My math decline was precipitous and comprehensive. Some years were worse than others; I managed to make it through fifth grade, but by seventh grade my father started discovering holes in my foundational math skills. It was hard to tell whether I had lost my head for numbers or just refused to absorb any math knowledge after the long-division fiasco, but one thing was clear: as my English developed, my math skills atrophied. My Russian accent faded, then disappeared, my vocabulary swelled, my command of idiom and slang became more supple, and my ability to grasp even elementary mathematical concepts disintegrated. Some years were better than others; I managed to acquit myself in algebra and trigonometry, but geometry and functions killed me. And in any given year, my father showed an uncanny ability to zero in on areas of weakness like a dentist poking right at the sensitive spot on a compromised tooth. In seventh grade, it was square roots. In geometry, it was my total inability to understand how to figure out the slope of a line (plus, I hated the teacher, a feeling I suspect was mutual). And in calculus, which my parents forced me to take—well, suffice it to say that I mostly didn't go to calculus because by then I had a driver's license and a car and enough free will to know that I would rather be shoe shopping at Vallco Fashion Center with fellow renegade Vivian Pham than listening to Mr. Axelrod drone on about how to calculate the volume of a revolving solid. My father made sporadic attempts to fill in the yawning gaps in my knowledge, and I resisted. He yelled; I cried. Late at night, after one particularly acrimonious session, my mother heard him muttering in his sleep, "The dog is buried under the root . . . the dog is buried under the root." "What root?" she asked, and he mumbled, "The square root."

And still, both my parents assumed that I would get over my dislike of math (and most science, for that matter) and become an engineer. It was the safe, logical, clear thing to do. Within a month of arriving in the United States, my mother had enrolled in community college and subsequently received an engineering degree; within two years of our arrival, both my parents were gainfully employed and making good money. Everyone in our family—uncles, aunts, several cousins—was an engineer. Despite the C that I received in physics my junior year or the fact that the only interest in engineering I ever evinced was in the key chains, adorable little pencils, and snow globes my father brought back from IEEE conventions, everyone assumed I would follow the same trodden path. My consistent and effortless A's in English went mostly unnoticed because what was the use of that? Ditto the A's in French. Ditto the fact that I began translating Bulgakov's *The Master and Margarita* in eleventh grade because I was dissatisfied with the two English language translations I had read.

In spite of my uneven grades (strong in the humanities, so-so in the sciences, let us not speak of the math), I managed to get into UCLA. My declared major at the time of application, in a half-hearted compromise that pleased no one, was international relations. I had adamantly refused to even consider engineering or the sciences, and my parents adamantly refused to allow me to consider English. International relations made sense because it was my mother's completely irrational hope that I would put my fluency in Russian to work as a diplomat or "do something in the foreign service." My father, meanwhile, held fast to the idea that in time, I would see the truth; I would, in spite of everything, recapture my glory days as a math prodigy and become an engineer.

And then, in spring of my freshman year, my seven-year-old cousin drowned in a freak accident on a family vacation in Mexico. It fell to my parents to drive to San Francisco and break the news to his grandmother and great-aunt and uncle, a fifty-mile drive that took over four hours because, as my mother later told me, they couldn't imagine how they would tell them that the smart, lively, laughing boy who was the first in the family to be born in the United States, who held such promise, who could be president one day, was dead, and so they kept pulling over and strolling aimlessly around, then driving the next couple of exits before stalling some more. It fell to my dad to pack up a plastic bin full of Benji's toys and carry it down to the garage because his mother, Irina, asked him to put them away before they returned. It fell to my parents to pick up Boris and Irina at the airport, to call me at UCLA, to ask me to come home for the funeral.

When the call came, I had been reading Toni Morrison's *Sula* and Geoffrey Chaucer's *The Canterbury Tales* simultaneously—*Sula* because my roommate asked for my help with a paper and I wanted to understand what the book was about; Chaucer because I had, on the sly, signed up for the introductory sequence for English majors. Chaucer and Morrison enthralled me for different reasons—Morrison for the raw, muscular, textured prose, for her unsparing descriptions of emotions and experiences totally alien to me, and Chaucer for the mind-boggling marriage of narrative sleight-of-hand and ribald humor (I had been reading "The Miller's Tale," little suspecting that it turned on one of the great dirty jokes of Western literature, and burst out laughing in the middle of the sunken quad across from Murphy Hall)—not to mention that guttural, juicy, German-inflected Middle English. It was like two voices were whispering in my head—one in Middle English, one in 1930s African American vernacular, but both saying the same thing: *This is why you came to college. This is what you were meant to do.*

After the funeral, I spent two more days at home and tried to fill the silence with stories. I recounted the clever twist piled upon clever twist at the brilliant end of "The Miller's Tale" and told my parents about how Sula, in the moment of her death, thinks of her best friend, Nell: "It didn't even hurt. Wait til I tell Nell." Maybe that's what happened to Benji, I said. Maybe it didn't even hurt.

Two weeks later, because we were all even more miserable apart than we were together and because they must have intuited that I wasn't eating, that I was waking in the middle of the night unable to go back to sleep, that I had started chain smoking, my parents came to visit me at UCLA. They took me grocery shopping, they sat in on some of my classes, and on their last smoggy, warm, blurred day in LA we walked on the beach in Santa Monica and my father skipped stones on the water. "Listen," he said, squinting into the setting sun and then turning to me. "I just want to tell you something. You don't have to be an engineer. The hell with engineering. You should study whatever you want."

It should have felt like a victory, but it did not. It felt like a somber, bitter, complicated blessing. My father was giving me permission to go do this thing he did not fully understand, where instead of making things with circuits and motherboards and numbers, you made things with words.

He was saying, go ahead and do this, even though none of us had any idea what the implications were. (Would I teach? Spend the next twenty years trying to write a novel? Wait tables?) Do this thing that is illogical, impractical, economically unsound, the thing that makes no sense—except that it made perfect sense, it added up, and both of us knew it.

▶ Please share an experience that made you feel uncomfortable or challenged, and then explain how you grew from the situation.

—GONZAGA UNIVERSITY

If we were never bewildered,
there would never be a story to tell about us.
—Henry James, *Art of the Novel*

My first official piece of identification was a birth certificate: *svidetelstvo o rozhdeniye*, a lilac booklet with the USSR seal—sheaves of wheat curving on either side of a hammer and sickle emblazoned over a globe. It states, in violet ink, that I was born on August 20, 1968, to Marcus Auerbuch, nationality Jew, and Svetlana Auerbuch, also a Jew. My second was an exit visa issued in 1977: a pale green rectangle with a black-and-white photo of me and my mother. In the photo, my mother is wearing a fuzzy angora sweater covered with swirling designs; I'm wearing a sweater under a jumper dress, my hair in pigtails held tight by ubiquitous Russian chiffon bows, my bangs cut in a severe line across my forehead. (You can't tell from the picture, but the swirls on my mother's sweater were beige, cream, and brown; the sweater under my navy jumper was traffic-cone orange.) The exit visa designates me as a Jew, traveling out of the USSR with my mother (also a Jew) for permanent residency in Israel due to religious reasons. This last part was a transparent falsehood: we were neither religious nor were we planning to settle in Israel, but this was not something to be disclosed in applying to leave the Soviet Union during the Cold War years, so all Jewish émigrés pretended that they were going to Israel, and the Soviet Union pretended to believe them.

Here the paperwork gets more complicated: once they applied to emigrate, my parents and I were designated enemies of the people, lost our Soviet citizenship, and became stateless. After the US government took us in, we became refugees seeking political asylum. In the United States, I received a California ID (where my first name was inexplicably spelled "Irine" and where my bangs are considerably longer and I am smiling giddily because, unlike dour Russians, Americans smiled all the time and encouraged others to do so as well). Two years after that, we received green cards, which were actually cream-colored and which designated us as residential aliens with the right to reside permanently in the United States. In three more years, we became eligible to apply for US citizenship, but here my father began to drag his feet. He liked not owing allegiance to a specific country. We were citizens of the world, he said. There was no hurry.

But it turned out we would have done well to hurry because in the summer of 1984, I got kicked out of Europe.

Every summer, the world history teachers from my high school, Mr. Fulcher and Mr. Crump, led a group of students on a trip to Europe. The trip had an ambitious itinerary—London, Paris, Salzburg, Vienna, and the Austrian countryside, covered by boat, bus, and train over three weeks. Everything was planned, every eventuality accounted for. Mr. Fulcher and Mr. Crump, gray-haired and avuncular, had done this trip at least a dozen times. But they never had a student like me, and what they—and my parents—didn't know to ask was whether I would require any additional paperwork. The US Citizenship and Immigration Services office had issued me a beige booklet, called a re-entry permit, which identified me as a 5'1", brown-haired, brown-eyed, fifteen-year-old female residential alien with the right to return to the United States, and everyone assumed that this was all I needed to travel abroad.

I found out the hard way that it wasn't when we landed in London's Heathrow Airport. My classmates sailed through passport control, nonchalantly flashing their dark blue and gold passports at the customs agents. When my turn came, I proudly displayed my re-entry permit—an object that had been passed from hand to hand on the plane, with much oohing and aahing about how interesting and exotic I was, how cool to be a citizen of no country instead of boringly American. The British customs official who examined my re-entry permit with a mixture of perplexity and disdain did not seem to share this admiration. As a stateless person with no citizenship, I would need a visa to enter the United Kingdom. I had no visa. For a few harrowing minutes, it appeared I would be turned around right then and there, until the agent studied my crestfallen face. "Just a second," he told me. Then he disappeared. Five minutes later, he returned with an emergency visa that allowed me to remain with my group in London for our three-day stay—seventy-two hours, he specified—as long as I didn't attempt to seek employment or establish permanent residency. Mr. Fulcher, shaken and considerably less jovial than he had been on the plane, assured him that I would do no such thing and then, as soon as we checked into our hotel and dropped off our bags, took me to the American embassy while the rest of my giddy classmates went sightseeing with Mr. Crump.

At the American embassy, we learned that none of the other countries on our itinerary would admit me without a visa, that I was lucky I was even allowed into England, and that the best course of action seemed to be to put me on a plane back to the United States after our stay in London was over. And so, after some desultory sightseeing with the rest of the group—irreparably tainted by my knowledge that my hours in Europe were numbered—I returned home four days after leaving, humiliated and heartbroken.

About eight months later, I wrote about the experience for a national writing contest. The story practically wrote itself; plus, it gave me an opportunity to exorcise the demons of my traumatic expulsion and to exercise my sardonic sixteen-year-old wit in railing against the arbitrary, impersonal cruelty of bureaucratic rules.

I opened the essay with what I believed at the time to be a wildly original move: an epigraph from the Merriam-Webster Collegiate Dictionary's definition of border. ("Bor • der: *n.* 1. the part or edge of a surface or area that forms its outer boundary. 2. the line that separates one country, state, province, etc., from another; frontier line.") Then came foreshadowing: I described the travel agency where we met to plan the trip, its walls plastered with the cheerful iconography of international adventure—bright posters of barges on the Danube, snow caps on the Swiss Alps, the soaring curve of the Eiffel Tower. Then symbolism: I described waiting in limbo on the wrong side of the gate as the dubious customs official turned my beige booklet in his hands and my classmates waited on the other side. I invoked the injustice of it all with Shylockian plangency: "To all appearances, we were the same," I wrote. "(All right, maybe I was a little bit shorter.) We spoke the same language, listened to the same music, laughed at the same jokes, took the same classes, looked forward to the trip with equal enthusiasm. And yet I was stateless and my classmates were not; I was a bureaucratic anomaly and they were not." And I concluded on an elegiac note, expressing the hope that in spite of the necessary borders between countries, there didn't have to be borders between people.

I wanted to call the essay "How I Spent My Summer," but my parents convinced me it was too cliché and I called it "Notes of a Traveler" instead, a title that strikes me to this day as belabored and not entirely accurate. (Then again, so is "How I Spent My Summer," given that my sojourn to Europe was all of seventy-two hours long, give or take.) No matter: the contest judges ate it up. I won a state-level prize.

What I didn't write about was this: the night before I was supposed to leave London, I went with Donna and Andrea, my hotel roommates, to a nearby corner store where, in open defiance of the rules of the trip, I bought a bottle of something amber-colored, potent-looking, and cheap. After all, as Donna pointed out, what were our teachers going to do if I were caught—send me home? Ha ha. Also, I bought an expensive, ill-fitting, itchy cable-knit wool sweater in an unflattering shade of oatmeal because I understood that you were supposed to buy wool in England and I reasoned that since I was going home the next day, I may as well spend as much money as possible, as quickly as possible. And although I had not, up to that point, been a particularly rebellious teenager (I snuck the occasional cigarette and, one time in eighth grade, held a thermometer to a lightbulb to fake a fever so I could stay home to watch *General Hospital*, but that was about it), buying liquor on a school trip seemed like the thing to do when you were getting kicked out of the country for having improper paperwork, just like buying a wool sweater was the thing to do when in England. And anyway, it was going to be just the three of us, me and Andrea and Donna, cozily getting drunk in our hotel room and collectively feeling sorry for me, except that stupid Scott

Cartwright, whose room was just down the hall, ended up inviting himself to my pity party.

The illicit drinking proceeded apace—for a while, the four of us just sat around, passing the bottle and repeating how much it sucked that I had to go home the next day—but what I hadn't counted on was that after enough drinking, we would somehow end up in a tangled heap on Andrea's bed. Things happened in surreal slow motion after that, things I only dimly remember but enough to know I'm not proud of them. Not the four-tongued, sixteen-limbed, forty-fingered Kama Sutra-esque orgy some of my classmates later insisted took place, but a lot of sloppy kissing and awkward groping in various configurations and Donna ending up without her shirt. There was nothing particularly erotic about any of it—Scott may have had a crush on me, but it was not a crush I reciprocated, and in the end, we were just four inexpert, drunken teenagers thrown together in a foreign country, one of them churning with a complex admixture of shame and sadness and betrayal, although by whom or what I could not say.

I woke up early the next morning to the tinny digital rendition of "Für Elise" issuing from my Armitron wristwatch. My eyes burned; I had a pounding headache, a sour stomach, and a mouth that tasted like something dead. When I looked in the mirror in the shared bathroom at the end of our hotel hallway, I hardly recognized the pale, blotchy face and kohl-smeared eyes as my own. I looked, yes, like an alien.

Donna was still sleeping, one naked arm poking above the mess of bedclothes, and Andrea gave me a half-hearted wave from her bed without meeting my eyes as I left our room. Because the rest of the group had to get on the London to Dover train to make the ferry crossing to France later that morning, I had to be at Heathrow no later than 8:00 a.m., which meant I would spend eight hours alone at the airport waiting for my late afternoon flight. Mr. Crump, who was clearly trading off with Mr. Fulcher in the burdensome task of dealing with me, took me to the airport by cab. He avoided meeting my eyes (probably because he felt bad about ditching me at the airport and not because he had somehow learned of the tawdry doings of the previous night, though I couldn't know that for sure). At the security checkpoint, he gave me an awkward hug and said he was so very sorry that things (things!) turned out that way and that he was absolutely certain I would return to Europe under happier circumstances. I gave him a wan smile, trying to conceal how much I hated him and everyone else on the trip and myself most of all, and went into the terminal.

At my gate, a ticket agent tried to put me on a plane to LA (which she called "Los Angelees") instead of San Francisco ("But it's in California, love," she kept saying, as though I were an idiot). Once I convinced her that Los Angeles and San Francisco were different cities hundreds of miles apart and secured a seat on a San Francisco-bound flight, I hunched down in a plastic bucket seat, nursing the first, and probably the worst, hangover of my life.

It wasn't so much the physical symptoms I minded as the disorienting sense of being utterly adrift—nauseated, head throbbing, about to cross an ocean for the second time in seventy-two hours. And even though I was being sent home because I didn't have the right paperwork, not because I had gotten drunk and screwed around in a hotel room, in my mind the two had become inextricably conflated.

At some point that afternoon, it occurred to me that I should probably call my parents—something I had avoided doing for the previous four days—because somehow telling them what had happened would make it real. But now there was no escaping reality, so I found a payphone and, after wrestling with international access codes and calling cards, placed the call to Sunnyvale, where it was one thirty in the morning. And when my mother's sleepy, anxious voice cut through the static, I burst into tears.

I had planned to be snide and funny—"You know how dad always goes on about how great it is to be a citizen of the world? Well, get this . . ."—but when I opened my mouth, all that came out, amid a lot of strangled sobbing, were the words "kicked out . . . visa . . . coming home." It took my mother several tries to understand what I was saying, that "coming home" meant imminently, in less than twenty-four hours, and once she got the gist of what I was trying to say, she calmed me down enough to get the flight number and arrival time. We hung up, and I disconsolately wiped my nose, trying to ignore the curious stares of other passengers.

On that endless June day in Heathrow, as the gray, dismal morning dripped moment by moment into a gray, dismal afternoon, it seemed like nothing would ever be right again. Somehow, I had wandered into terra incognita, beyond recognizable boundaries of any kind. It wasn't just that I was shuttling between countries, stuck in limbo in the international terminal at Heathrow; it was that I had no idea where I belonged or who I was. Much later, in graduate school, I would acquire the vocabulary that might have come close to describing how I felt—*extraterritorial, marginal, liminal*—but for now, my lacerating inner monologue was much less sophisticated. I was an idiot. Certainly, I was no longer a good girl. Good girls made sound decisions and did not get drunk in hotel rooms with boys they didn't even like all that much. Good girls were good citizens.

My essay also skipped over the trip's aftermath: after our drunken debauchery, Scott came staggering back to his hotel room late that night and confided in his roommates, who in turn confided in everyone else on the trip, amplifying salacious details like an X-rated game of telephone. Once they all returned to our sleepy corner of Silicon Valley suburbia, the news spread like wildfire. I was determined to ignore Scott completely and to stay entirely mum, but the ignoring part turned out to be harder than I thought: in an ironic twist, Scott and I were placed in the same junior-year American Literature class, where the first assigned novel, and I am not making this up, was Nathaniel Hawthorne's *The Scarlet Letter*.

Yes, that *Scarlet Letter*—the one in which Hester Prynne, the original bad girl in the American literary canon, does unspeakable things in the forest with the village minister, gets pregnant, bears an out-of-wedlock child, and is made to wear a scarlet "A" as a punishment for her transgressions. The hierarchies of shame in high school are at least as complex and unforgiving as those in an eighteenth-century Puritan hamlet, and though my own petty transgressions lacked the mythic scope and heft of Hester's, I may as well have worn a scarlet "S," for slut, all through the fall of my junior year. The sideways glances and lopsided smiles and whispers that trailed me like smoke said as much, though I did not want to be a slut and did not think of myself as a slut. Aside from Scott, I had kissed maybe two or three other boys and had indulged in some not particularly heavy petting at summer camp. And because I lacked the kind of courage that stiffened Hester's spine on the scaffold and drove her to embroider the ornate "A" on her breast with desperate ostentation, I hid inside baggy sweaters (though the sweater I bought in London sat unworn in my closet) and skulked away when someone let slip a snide comment about "that Europe trip." But Hester and I had this in common: she for years, and I for several long months, existed beyond the pale of every social circle. Hester had her sewing, and of course little Pearl, to occupy her time; I brought books to school so that I had something to do when I sat by myself at lunch.

And then, as usually happens, the titillating summer gossip was supplanted by more exciting news—most notably, a cheating scandal where an enterprising senior was raking in $400 a pop to take the SAT for other people—and slowly, I was reintegrated into the social fabric of high school. By Halloween, "what happened on the Europe trip" was old news. And in November of my junior year, my parents and I received our citizenship. (Impelled by my aborted foray into Europe, my parents completed the citizenship application within a week of my return.) The swearing-in felt strangely vindicating and also surreal; a few months before, I had been nobody and belonged nowhere, and now I was being strenuously welcomed into something the presiding judge called "the American family." And yet I was no different coming out of the swearing-in ceremony than I had been going in, except that now I had a certificate of naturalized citizenship and could apply for a blue and gold booklet that entitled me to travel the world without impediment and did not, in any way, reflect the content of my character or my moral worth. Plus, I had recently received an equally important document: a driver's license granting me the freedom to roam the Sunnyvale and Cupertino area in my parents' beat-up 1973 Plymouth Satellite. The world was opening up.

Identity is a funny thing. By the time I received my US citizenship at sixteen, I had been a Soviet citizen, a refugee, a residential alien, and (briefly) the slut of Homestead High School. At my Catholic middle school, I was taunted for being a "Jewish communist," which was only half true, as my parents and I left the Soviet Union before I had even gotten to be a Young Pioneer.[11] The one that felt truest, the one I felt in my bones, was the notification I got in November 1985 that I had won the National Council of Teachers of English

11. I'm still a little bit mad about that. Mostly it's being denied the red scarf I'd get to wear around my neck that galls me. I was so close—mere weeks away!—and now it's forever out of my reach.

writing contest. I had a feeling, while I was writing the essay in a white heat earlier that fall, that the straw of my European fiasco could be spun into narrative gold, and it turned out I was right. I had staked out new territory and discovered the pleasures of narrative discrimination, of shaping the world in a way that made sense to me, of building for myself, however tenuous, a house of words. I was a writer.

▶ Reflect on something that someone has done for you that has made you happy or thankful in a surprising way. How has this gratitude affected or motivated you?

—COMMON APPLICATION PERSONAL STATEMENT PROMPT

It was smoking that brought us together. At least that's what I like to tell people who ask how David and I met, although technically, we first met when we were twelve and my parents enrolled me in Hebrew school at Temple Beth Am midway through the school year and the teacher walked me into the classroom and triumphantly announced, "Irena is a recently arrived Soviet émigré," and everyone stared at me unblinkingly and I wanted to disappear from the face of the earth.

I lasted about two months at Beth Am. At the time, I was attending St. Lawrence Academy on the recommendation of our Irish Catholic neighbors in Sunnyvale while staying up late reading Leon Uris' *Exodus* and *Mila-18* and Herman Wouk's *The Winds of War* and Ruth Gruber's *Raquela: A Woman of Israel.* This made me confusing to my Beth Am classmates, whose bland indifference to the horrors visited upon the Jewish people was equally confusing to me. My attendance dwindled, then stopped before the school year was even over; four years later, David—whose presence in the Beth Am classroom I had not even registered—came up to me during passing period at Homestead High and reminded me that we had briefly attended Hebrew school together. I grimaced, because that was not a part of my life I particularly cared to remember, and that was that.

But then, senior year, our paths began to intersect. He was the TA in my French class, and he began leaving little notes on the quizzes and homework assignments he had graded: "*Tu as une grande bouche*" was one, accompanied by a smiley face with a rakish swoop on top. We were in the same legendary senior course, War and Peace, where the teacher, Rodger Halstead, whom everyone called Rodg, assigned articles that examined violence through psychological, evolutionary, and anthropological perspectives, where the air was heady with intellectual ferment, where we shouted at each other about nature and nurture, the moral right—or lack thereof—of the Israelis to displace the Palestinians, and the Stanford prison experiment, and where David and I began to lock eyes for increasingly longer periods of time.

In Nabokov's last Russian language novel, *The Gift*, Fyodor, the main character, marvels at fate's numerous attempts to connect him and Zina, who turns out to be his true love. According to Fyodor, fate—exasperated by multiple missed connections—finally pushes the two of them together in a clumsy, clearly contrived maneuver. In our case, fate operated through Philip Morris.

As I was about to walk through the gate to the school parking lot for the last time as a graduating senior—the cap and gown had been picked up, the locker cleaned out—I saw David heading in the same direction, and I realized with stunning clarity that if I walked past him I would never see him again and, because I couldn't very well say, "Please don't walk out of my life forever!" I said, "Come have a cigarette with me." And even though David was not a smoker, he agreed.

In 1986, it was illegal for anyone under eighteen to buy cigarettes, but not, apparently, for a high school to have a designated smoking section for its students. So we sat together on a low, putty-colored wall and talked for nearly two hours about nothing and everything, and I bullied David into taking me to see *Hannah and Her Sisters* even though I had already seen it, and on the way to the theater he was so nervous that he drove over the curb at Palo Alto Square, and even though doing so is a critical offense on a behind-the-wheel exam, I gave him a pass. And thus our story began.

About a week after *Hannah and Her Sisters*, David sent me a Far Side card depicting neon-colored dinosaurs smoking cigarettes. The caption said, "The real reason dinosaurs became extinct." Inside, he had written, "Every breath you take is important, as Sting might say." And I thought to myself, *Hmm*. Then I found a card and wrote him back.

Our summer romance felt exactly like what the Master tells Ivan Bezdomny about his romance with Margarita: "Love leaped out in front of us like a murderer in an alley leaping out of nowhere, and struck us both at once. As lightning strikes, as a Finnish knife strikes." It came out of nowhere; it left us both breathless. We *got* each other, even when we were being insufferably snotty, even when I gloated that I got a 5 on the AP English Literature exam while David only got a 4, or when David would ask what I got on the AP Calculus exam (nothing, because I didn't take it, *David*). I made David watch *Annie Hall*, and we quoted from it endlessly. When he left for Cornell and I went to UCLA, we wrote letters, sometimes several a week. We drew pictures of campus buildings and talked about books we were reading in our classes and pined after each other and fell into each other's arms every break and every summer. We worked at the same summer camp, where David made me elaborate lanyards and we regaled our campers with our best Miracle

Max and Valerie imitations from *The Princess Bride*. During the school year, I sent David my Shakespeare notes because he had a crappy Shakespeare professor (so much for an Ivy League school) and I had a phenomenal one—Seth Wiener, who in spite of a severe stutter, made Shakespeare come alive and sing in a way that no one has before or since—and both of us swooned over the dark music of *Macbeth* and *Othello*. We sent each other mix tapes and poems; when we were apart, I spent hours listening to Berlin's "Take My Breath Away" on repeat. I whispered, ". . . nobody, not even the rain, has such small hands," to myself while tracing David's crabbed writing, half script, half print.

Cigarette paper is a flimsy thing, designed to smolder slowly and turn to ash. But paper with markings on it—that endures. In *The Master and Margarita*, the Master, terrified that he will be arrested by the Soviet authorities for writing a novel about Pontius Pilate, burns his manuscript in the stove. Later, the manuscript miraculously reappears, restored by the devil, who, in one of the most celebrated lines in Russian literature, tells the Master that manuscripts don't burn. And while our letters may have been a pale substitute for the heat and urgency of physical presence, they became a way for us to lay ourselves bare, to make ourselves known to each other. So much so that, like any good epistolary novel, what began with the post office ended with a church[12]—or, in our case, the Gold Room in San Francisco's Fairmont Hotel.

12. I'm indebted for this description to Nabokov's *The Gift*, where he describes a street "beginning with a post office and ending with a church, like an epistolary novel."

PART TWO
COMPLICATIONS

▶ Discuss an accomplishment, event, or realization that sparked a period of personal growth and a new understanding of yourself and others.

—COMMON APPLICATION PERSONAL STATEMENT PROMPT

The wedding dress I wanted more than anything else in the world was dead simple: an off-the-shoulder, sleeveless white sheath with a veil that was nothing more than a mother of pearl pin that anchored in my hair and trailed a length of tulle down to the ground. But the year before David and I got married, I developed urticaria—hives that would appear all over my chest and arms whenever I became stressed or overheated—so the wedding dress I got was an elaborate concoction with a nipped-in waist and a voluminous skirt and a complicated bustle that took three people to assemble and netting over the chest and arms that was meant to camouflage the red welts that would certainly appear on my chest and arms as soon as the wedding got going.[13]

David and I were twenty-one when we got married, and one of our friends remarked that our wedding felt like

13. Two weeks before the wedding, I figured out that taking an antihistamine beforehand would preempt the hives, but by then it was too late and the perfect wedding dress, like the scarlet Young Pioneer scarf, is now forever out of my reach.

senior prom. And maybe we did feel more like children than adults when, after checking in at a B&B on the way to UCLA where David would start medical school and I would start graduate school, we called our parents from our room, to just, you know, make sure that it was okay for us to be there.

When we moved into our apartment on Midvale Avenue, we didn't know to call ahead and get the power turned on, and for the first night, we slept on the floor in sleeping bags in a dark apartment. The next day we went to Stør, the precursor of IKEA, and bought furniture with whimsical Swedish names—the SVALKA table, the BREMEN couch. I discovered that David was organized to a fault: on day five of our marriage, he remarked casually that I put the cream cheese on the wrong shelf again because apparently it impeded his ability to easily get the milk. Until that moment, I had not realized there *was* a right shelf for the cream cheese, but it was hard to hold a grudge against someone who was adept at assembling cheap Swedish furniture and remembered to water the plants and made me laugh on a regular basis and introduced me to *Star Trek: The Next Generation*—in particular, to an episode called "Darmok," where Captain Picard, in order to make himself understood to an alien species that communicates only in metaphor, tells the story of Gilgamesh and Enkidu. We bought a bougainvillea for our balcony and studied together in the living room. When David brought home an assortment of human bones for his gross anatomy course, I arranged them artistically on our pine RIKKI coffee table and sketched them with a blue crayon. Occasionally, we'd have a massive fight, usually about something trivial; in one particularly acrimonious instance, David took offense at my description of the corn tortillas he bought as "mealy" and stormed from the table, and it wasn't until the Random House College Dictionary convinced him that in calling the tortillas mealy

I was referring to their texture, not to some worm-ridden quality, that we reconciled.

In the mornings, David and I would walk to campus while I pointed out architectural curiosities throughout Westwood Village ("look at the curved molding under those windows—you could totally sleep there if you had a fight with your roommate!") and the fact that Arby's was open at 8:00 a.m. (seriously, who eats roast beef at that hour?) and David would grunt in response (I am a morning person; he is not). The other graduate students in Comp Lit were funny and congenial and we hung out in the TA lounge and one of my fellow TA's pilfered my teaching copy of *The Decameron* and signed it "To my good friend Irena. From, G. Boccaccio" in red ballpoint pen. I loved teaching; I loved sitting around seminar tables in my Goodwill men's blazer and long flowy skirts and Doc Martens discussing female archetypes and narrative desire and Slavoj Zizek. I loved holding forth to freshmen about the importance of hospitality in *The Odyssey* and the conflation of writing and desire in *Les Liaisons Dangereuses*. I loved smoking on the third-floor terrace of Royce Hall, blowing smoke rings and gossiping about the newest department hire, who was spotted carrying around a gallon jug of Gallo white wine at the most recent Comp Lit party as though it were a purse.

Except for one thing: to live in Los Angeles is to willfully disregard that everything is built on a shifting foundation, that everything can crumble in a moment. There was catastrophic flooding our first winter, and in spring of 1991, Santa Ana winds—known also as devil winds—blew furnace-hot from the desert and rattled magnolia leaves and started fires and, in the words of Raymond Chandler, caused meek little wives to finger the edge of the carving knife and eye their husbands' necks. (Not me, though. I liked my husband just fine.) It was also in 1991 that we watched, horrified, as a grainy, black-and-white video showed four white police officers raining their batons down on a prone Black man. In 1992, LA exploded into a paroxysm of fire and blood after a jury acquitted three of the officers and failed to reach a verdict on the fourth. Four young Black men beat a white truck driver to a pulp on the corner of Florence and Normandie, all of it broadcast on national television from circling helicopters. Ash rained from the sky, the air smelled like smoke throughout the city, and everything felt irreparably broken.

I first learned the word *chthonic* as a TA for Katherine King, a classics professor who had wild white shoulder-length hair and dressed in baggy linen pants and lived in a bungalow in Venice Beach whose porch was decorated with a sticker that read "Subvert the Dominant Paradigm." She was famous for hurling grapes at the provost during a comp lit reception because she wanted to express her solidarity with the United Farm Workers, and I was a little bit afraid of her. When she lectured, she became incandescent; I could easily imagine her in a body-length peplos, her hair twined with a garland of laurel, or perhaps writhing with snakes. I never doubted I should be studying contemporary literature until I heard her speak; she taught *The Oresteia* as though Agamemnon, Clytemnestra, Cassandra, Electra, and Iphigeneia were known to her. Even the freshmen, who were taking the class only to fulfill the humanities and composition requirement, were spellbound when she talked about the stand-off between the Olympian and the chthonic gods in *The Eumenides*. The Olympian gods presided over reason, logic, learning, daylight. The chthonic gods dwelt in the darkness; their domain was blood, birth, the twisting roots beneath the surface, vengeance. And because I was young and cocky and had already forgotten what it meant to suffer, I loved how it all sounded. I whispered *chthonic* to myself, relishing the click of the hard "ch" in the back of my throat, the hissing "th" against the front teeth.

▶ Describe the most significant challenge you have faced and the steps you have taken to overcome this challenge.

—UNIVERSITY OF CALIFORNIA PERSONAL INSIGHT QUESTION

Jordan was conceived shortly before the 1994 Northridge earthquake, and I always wondered afterward if our first crack at conceiving a child literally caused the earth to move. The earthquake hit at 4:30 a.m. on January 17, knocking out electricity, wantonly throwing books off our shelves—Jane Austen's *Sense and Sensibility*, Slavoj Zizek's *The Sublime Object of Ideology*, *Grant's Atlas of Anatomy*, *The MLA Guide for Writers of Research Papers*—and setting off every car alarm in the greater LA area. Neither David nor I were in the least prepared. For ostensibly smart people who were getting advanced degrees, we were pretty stupid: we had no flashlight, no battery-operated radio, no shoes by the bed. When the shaking stopped and we ventured out of our bedroom, we cut our bare feet on broken glass, then lit candles to assess the damage. We were lucky—the damage was minimal, and in addition to being spared from heavy falling objects, exploding gas lines, contaminated drinking water, and house fires, I got pregnant. Practically on the first try.

Nine months later, nearly to the day, Jordan entered the world via semi-emergency C-section after a twelve-hour labor during which it became manifestly apparent that my uterus was incapable of expelling him on its own. In hospital parlance, this was called "failure to progress," so in came my OB, trailing a battery of surgical nurses and residents in her wake, and minutes later, Jordan, with his head out and his body still in my abdominal cavity, took his first breath and uttered his first mewling cry. The noise was so jarring in that otherwise hushed operating room that I asked David if that was the baby. David, seated by my head in surgical scrubs, said, "Well, duh," with unaccustomed tenderness and squeezed my hand. "Of course it's the baby," cooed my OB as she stitched layers of muscle and skin back together and a pediatrics resident took Jordan's vital signs in the corner. "Look at that little butterball."

Four days later, we dressed the little butterball in a yellow onesie embroidered with ducks, slipped on a matching hat, inserted him awkwardly into a car seat, and took him home. I sat on our living room couch, holding a sleeping Jordan and sobbing because I was exhausted and in pain and couldn't believe that the hospital would let us bring a baby home, just like that, and here we were completely clueless about how to take care of him. And thus our life as new parents began.

Between Jordan's conception and birth, two things happened and one did not. David graduated from medical school, and I completed my PhD qualifying exams. But in spite of a substantial dissertation-year fellowship, I did not write my dissertation. I didn't even pretend to write my dissertation. While David began his psychiatry residency at Stanford, I swam laps in the local community center pool, cooked chicken saltimbocca, and, in a misguided attempt at nesting, bought some hideous wrought-iron candelabra at Z Gallerie. The candelabra were not returnable, and David wondered out loud why some nesting women scrub woodwork and wash windows while others feather the nest with nonreturnable wrought-iron monstrosities that look like they would be at home in Dracula's castle. The answer was simple: I didn't know what to do with myself, and the obvious solution—to get to work on the dissertation, immediately, *now, this minute*, as everyone who had children suggested I do—was impossible, as I refused to set foot in the library.

I thought my refusal made perfect sense. Although I had practically lived in the library during my years at UCLA, I now had ample reason to avoid the Stanford library—ample being the operative word. I was embarrassed. Embarrassed to walk into the hushed, red-carpeted lobby or to squeeze through the narrow stacks with my belly preceding me by a good foot and my belly button poking through my dowdy maternity top like a plastic timer on a store-bought turkey. I was embarrassed to be seen on a college campus at all. I had gone and gotten myself knocked up, and now that the evidence was in full view—well, that was pretty much it for my life as an academic.

To complicate matters, when the fellowship was awarded, I was pregnant but not yet showing, skinny and smart, the darling of the Comp Lit department, an exemplary student without a single incomplete, a teaching assistant universally acknowledged by faculty to be one of the finest in recent memory, admired by (most) fellow grad students, beloved by (most) undergrads, a recent Russian émigré whose dissertation—on displacement and semantic instability in the works of Henry James and Vladimir Nabokov, themselves expats and emigres—promised to make of her own exile a thing of beauty. I was on the fast track to academic superstardom, a wunderkind, the student our chair liked to point to when asked about time-to-degree and other ticklish questions by prospective applicants. Now I had grown big with child and become exiled—forever, it seemed—from the ranks of literary and literate anorexics to which I desperately wanted to belong. My dissertation advisor was serenely chic and rail thin and had no children; so was Ruth Yeazell, who taught the Virginia Woolf seminar. A life of the mind, it seemed, was not compatible with the life of the body.

Mine, however, was fast becoming a life of the body. At barely 5'1", I was quite literally subsumed by my pregnancy. My new shape—all belly and breasts—began to attract attention from relatives, friends, acquaintances, strangers in the supermarket. Only recently, it seemed, I had been in Kathy Komar's feminist theory seminar discussing ways in which the female body, in literature and in life, was objectified, fetishized, commodified, subjugated by the patriarchal gaze (though not *my* body, thank you very much), and now it was happening to me. I became the object of other narratives—of conjecture, jokes, criticism, unwanted confidences, unsolicited advice. People I didn't know—or certainly didn't know well enough—asked me how much weight I had gained, remarked on my size and shape (too big, too pointy, too round, about to burst), told me not to lift heavy grocery bags, swim, take hot showers, eat sweets, bend to the side, walk too fast or too far. Get as much sleep as possible now, they said. You're not getting any sleep when the baby comes, that's for sure. Oh, and sex too, ha ha! And finish your dissertation, finish it *now.* Because after you have that baby, your life will never be the same again.

I scoffed. It was painfully obvious that David and I were nothing like the pathetic people who pressed their advice on us (mostly me). We had advanced degrees; we had worked as summer camp counselors. Surely we would manage to lead fulfilled lives, pursuing our own interests while nurturing and molding our little one; surely we could get our child to sleep through the night. Of course it was going to be tough going for a few days after he was born, but then we would settle into a domestic routine in which David went off to the hospital while I, cooing baby serenely cradled against my breast, completed my dissertation and landed a plum tenure-track job somewhere in the Bay Area.

Our learning curve after we brought Jordan home was steep. We learned, among other things, that newborns never sleep and that it is impossible to write a dissertation, or anything else for that matter, up to and including a grocery list, with one in the house. We spent the first months of Jordan's life dazed, living from crisis to crisis. Everything leaked—diapers, breast milk, spit up, tears. I cried nonstop, because on some days my crowning achievement was a shower and a bowl of instant oatmeal by late afternoon: because there were no adults to talk to, because I was still carrying most of my pregnancy weight and clearly getting stupider with each passing day, because I was never going to finish my dissertation. Never, never, never.

We tried a nanny, Lena, who had recently arrived from St. Petersburg and was available Monday, Tuesday, and Thursday mornings. The arrangement was doomed from the beginning. In our 800-square-foot rental, I could hear every sound she and Jordan made as she gurgled to him in Russian (one of her selling points) and I stared dully at a blank computer screen, overwhelmed by guilt and inertia. The dissertation was going nowhere fast. Like Jordan's birthing process, both it and I seemed to be suffering from a failure to progress, and on top of everything, I acquired—overnight, it seemed—what Henry James called "an imagination of disaster." Lena would take Jordan for a stroller walk, and I would envision scenarios in which she tripped and spilled him out on the sidewalk or a stranger grabbed him or she dropped dead from a heart attack in the middle of the street, leaving him alone and helpless.

For all her good intentions, Lena was not helping much, which was probably my fault more than hers. Plus, she had opinions and ideas, some of which, to put it charitably, were a little eccentric. She bundled Jordan in so many layers when they went out that it looked like they were setting out for the North Pole. Every time he fussed, she claimed his stomach was bothering him. One day, she noted in passing that he never looked straight at her. "I try to catch his eye," she said, "and he just looks straight through me. Or he looks away. Have you had his vision checked?"

We had not had his vision checked. David was on call every fourth night, and his pager beeped incessantly even when he wasn't. Neither of us had had a full night's sleep for months. We were subsisting on frozen dinners and cheap takeout and having screaming fights four to five times a week and since none of our friends had gotten around to having children, we had no peer group, no point of comparison.

In desperation, I joined a mom-and-baby group at Stanford. But at twenty-six, I was a good five years younger than the youngest of the moms, who seemed to actually be enjoying motherhood and who had it together enough to stop by Starbucks and grab a latte before the group, while I could barely wrestle Jordan into his car seat. Their babies sat placidly on their baby blankets and babbled and smiled and perused board books and played with toys; Jordan crawled inexorably toward the open door every time I loosened my grip on him. Being in the mom and baby group made me feel stupid and incompetent; trying to write made me feel stupid and incompetent; when I took Jordan to the playground, I felt like an outright misanthrope. The other mothers would squeal, "Good job going down the slide!" at their children, and I would cast dark looks at them and think, "It's called gravity, for the love of Jesus."

At his wits' end, David floated the idea of placing Jordan

in part-time daycare, provoking our most spectacular screaming match to date. "Why even have children," I sobbed at the kitchen table, "if you're just going to farm them out to be raised by other people?"

But gradually, grudgingly, I had to admit that David was right. We let Lena go and found a spot at Stanford's daycare center, where a meticulous Frenchwoman named Yvet presided beneficently over Jordan and five of his colleagues. And it turned out that Virginia Woolf was right—all I needed, really, was a room of my own. I would drop off Jordan, come home, barricade myself behind stacks of books, and write, and write, and write. I lived on a steady diet of coffee and Hershey's miniatures left over from Halloween (oddly, that and the intellectual exertion seemed to do the trick that diet and exercise could not), and as I grew slimmer, the dissertation took on shape and heft. And then it was done, all 283 pages of it, not including the acknowledgments, where I thanked my parents, who had brought me to America,[14] and David, who had brought America to me (in truth, I was plenty Americanized already, but I couldn't resist the syllepsis). I also mentioned what a delight it was to watch Jordan learn and grow as I worked on the dissertation.

Technically, this last part was not entirely accurate, but it seemed important to link bringing Jordan and the dissertation into the world at roughly the same time. It had a pleasing narrative symmetry, capped off by the fact that I had landed a part-time humanities lectureship at Stanford beginning that fall. I had it all: an adorable toddler, a dissertation, and a teaching job. The end.

---

14. In addition to bringing me to America, they also watched Jordan so I could write, and my mother read most of the novels I was writing about in my dissertation—including *The Golden Bowl*, which is widely considered Henry James's most impenetrable novel. We both loved *Portrait of a Lady* and had heated arguments about *Washington Square* in which my mother insisted Dr. Sloper, Catherine's authoritarian father, was a good man who had her best interests at heart and I maintained that he was a controlling asshole.

Only it wasn't the end at all because while I was blithely writing about how exile impelled meaning-making in the lives and work of James and Nabokov, another narrative was unfolding right under our noses, marked by a nagging sense of something missing. It developed slowly at first, then faster, with the inexorability of a train picking up speed on a downward slope. Jordan was blond, round, dimpled, winsome. He met all the physical milestones and sat up, crawled, stood, and walked almost exactly on schedule. But—and this was a big "but"—something felt off, and it came down to this: we were not having much fun together.

At first we thought it was us—cerebral, neurotic, overeducated parents. We would go out on date night and end up in a bookstore, in the child development section, browsing through books like *Your Fun Toddler* and *Games Babies Play*. But somehow the rousing game of peekaboo that was a hit with the random toddler at the supermarket left Jordan cold. While other children in daycare squealed with delight when David or I walked in, Jordan remained unmoved. When we picked him up, he put his elbow into our necks and arched away. We didn't mean to compare Jordan to other children—okay, we did, constantly, but who doesn't?—but the truth was that he did not benefit from the comparison. Something was clearly very wrong. And in spite of the fact that we thought of ourselves (smugly, hubristically) as pretty smart people, we were entirely destitute of ideas.

▶ At UVM, learning extends far beyond the walls of our classrooms. From student-led organizations, to internships and study abroad experiences, UVM students are encouraged to pursue knowledge in all environments. Describe a time when you've learned in a nontraditional setting.

—UNIVERSITY OF VERMONT

When Jordan was barely two, my grandmother choked on a Danish and almost died. We were at Prolific Oven, a cozy-shabby bakery in downtown Palo Alto, which we patronized nearly every week. It was spacious enough to accommodate me, Jordan's stroller, an amply-proportioned septuagenarian, and multiple shopping bags.

Prolific Oven was an easy fifteen-minute stroll from Lytton Gardens, a senior community where Grandma Ester lived, and nearly equidistant from Ross Dress for Less, a sprawling discount store on University Avenue. We tried to hit Ross on Tuesdays, which were senior discount days, but sometimes we came on other days as well. If Grandma Ester found something she liked on an off day she would stash it in a secret location in hopes that it would remain untouched until the following Tuesday, when she could take advantage of the 10 percent discount. She found ingenious hiding places, stuffing a boisterously flowered dress into a pasta pot in housewares, wedging a billowing teal rayon blouse behind a rack of negligees. Most of the time, her treasures remained undisturbed until we returned, but on some days the pasta pot would be empty or the teal blouse would be missing from its lingerie hideout. On those days, she would mutter "*Vot gady*"—the bastards—and scour the racks for something else. If she found something that she thought might look good on me, she would press it on me with the fervor of an evangelist, and if I protested that I already had all the cardigans I needed, she would say in a stentorian voice, "*Takovo u tebya nyet.*" Like this one, you do not have.

Grandma Ester was given to epic excess and intensity—in her pronouncements, in her dress, and in her habits. She was bossy and histrionic. She played favorites. She pitted my mother and my aunt against each other with the skill of an experienced dogfighter. She dealt in superlatives—I was the best granddaughter until my younger cousin Inna usurped that title, and then the crown of the favorite shifted to Inna's much younger sister Becky's curly little head and stayed there for years. But when Becky was ten, I had Jordan, Grandma Ester's first great-grandchild, and the crown passed once again. Jordan, according to Grandma Ester, was the smartest, the best, the most amazing baby in the world.

Personally, I was worried that Jordan never pointed anything out or remarked on anything or asked questions, but she insisted that he was a genius. I wanted desperately for him to be a genius, but on most days just catching his eye seemed nearly impossible. He wasn't interested in being read to. He didn't understand that when someone rolled him a ball, he was expected to roll it back. He didn't seek out attention. He didn't seem particularly attached to me or David—or, really, to anyone.

At Prolific Oven, we always ordered the same thing:

two coffees, an enormous bear claw for Grandma Ester, and a croissant for me. Jordan had zero interest in table food, preferring instead the Cheerios I toted along in a plastic Tupperware. He grabbed them with an oddly clumsy, open-handed grasp and shoved them at his mouth.

When my grandmother choked on the Danish, I was in the middle of simultaneously asking her a question and picking up a toy Jordan dropped on the floor, so I wasn't looking at her. But after my query was met with silence, I looked up and saw immediately why she wasn't speaking. Her eyes were bulging, she was leaning forward intently, and she was waving her hands near her throat. Not even so much waving as convulsing—jerky, frantic movements I had never before seen another human being make and hope never to again. I didn't realize until then that the choking sign was universal, as much in the eyes as in the hands. It's a signal that says more than "I have something stuck in my throat." It says, clearly and unambiguously, "I am going to die."

I jumped out of my chair at the same time that she half-leapt, half-fell out of hers. Her chair clattered over; I got behind her and tried to wedge my arms around her oddly hard midsection. (After many years of accompanying her to doctor's appointments I would learn that she wore a corset-like longline bra in an effort to contain her waist, which accounted for the hardness.) But even with the corset, she was too big around, and my hands came nowhere near her sternum. And now she was collapsing, and I could do nothing.

Fortunately, the alert, multiple-pierced clerk behind the counter had longer arms than I did. After two vigorous thrusts, the offending piece of Danish shot out of my grandmother's mouth along with a dribble of vomit, and she dropped heavily into a chair, gasping.

Someone called 911, even though she was clearly in no further danger, and I thanked the clerk profusely. Grandma

Ester seemed angry more than anything else. She sullenly waved away the offer of a glass of water and said she didn't want the water or the paramedics, she just wanted to go home. My hands were shaking so hard that I had to squeeze them together. I bent down to retrieve the knocked-over chair and only then did I realize that in the midst of the commotion, Jordan had continued to sit placidly in the stroller, eating Cheerios.

At the time, I took little note of his calm detachment. If anything, it was convenient to have him sitting quietly in the stroller instead of thrashing around or crying or asking what was happening. On our glum walk home, my grandmother remarked what an extraordinary child he was. "Not a peep," she said. "He knew not to get in the way." But the more I thought about it, the more his indifference seemed ominous. What toddler could be so profoundly unmoved by what had just transpired? Then again, what toddler ignored toys and playmates in favor of the endless opening and closing of doors? Who arched away when hugged?

Seven months after the choking incident, we found out there was a name for what was wrong with Jordan. In the terrible, clear light of the diagnostic aftermath, his calm imperviousness at Prolific Oven turned out to be one of the many pieces that completed this particular puzzle—the lack of curiosity, the absence of spontaneous, expressive language, the impoverished range of emotions. He didn't react because all that sound and fury meant nothing to him. He should have been demanding attention, and pointing at things, and drinking in every detail of the world around him. Instead, it was Grandma Ester and I who were cramming in as much as possible—a new dress, an unneeded cardigan, a too-big piece of Danish. Jordan was pushing everything away, unmoving, unscathed, wholly self-contained, like the Cheerios in his snap-lock container.

I saw my grandmother differently after that. All of us—me, my parents, my aunt and uncle, my cousins—were always slightly cowed by her, but there was always a tinge of comedy to our fear. She was so bombastic, so over the top. But now her bluster was tinged with tragedy. She seemed diminished somehow. Vulnerable. Painfully mortal.

Our trips to Ross grew infrequent, and we avoided Prolific Oven by tacit agreement. And once Jordan was diagnosed, I was too consumed with trying to cram two years of missed development into him as quickly as possible to have time or energy for anything else.

Many years later, when we moved Grandma Ester into assisted living and cleaned out the Lytton Gardens apartment, we found dozens of clothes and accessories shoved in every available crevice. I recognized some from our Prolific Oven and Ross days; some of them had hardly been worn. Some still had tags attached.

We never told my grandmother about Jordan's diagnosis. Between her limited English and blind adoration, his language deficits were easy enough to minimize. As far as we know, she never caught on, although occasionally, during the first brutal years of intensive behavioral therapy, when we demanded Jordan's attention practically every minute, she would bark, "Why are you always torturing that poor child? Leave him alone!" And then, more softly: "You know I love all of you, but Jordan—well, Jordan is right here." And she would tap her heart, once, twice, three times. "There is no one else like him."

▶ Share an essay on a topic of your choice. It can be one you've already written, one that responds to a different prompt, or one of your own design.

—COMMON APPLICATION PERSONAL STATEMENT PROMPT

Title: How to Lose Weight Quickly and Effectively!

1.

Start[15] by feeling queasy for a few weeks—or, now that you think of it, months, really. Regret, not for the first or last time, that you quit smoking. Drink a lot of coffee (skim milk, no sugar) and fret about why your two-year-old doesn't eat anything except Cheerios and prodigious quantities of Ritz crackers smeared with peanut butter or drink anything but apple juice, and only from a purple sippy cup with a yellow

15. For those of you who keep track of such things: we're shifting into the literary present tense. Yes, what I'm describing belongs to the past, but the events that follow Jordan's diagnosis—and its repercussions—feel like they're still happening, will always be happening. Hence the literary present, which effectively freezes time.

When I began teaching humanities at UCLA, I realized that most of my students didn't understand what I knew intuitively: that Odysseus would *always* be trying to reach Ithaca, would *always* be driving the olive stake through the Cyclops' eye, would *always* be slaughtering the suitors. Tess would *always* be lying on the sacrificial stone at Stonehenge. Humbert would forever be grasping at his kingdom by the sea and forever watching it slip through his fingers. Mrs. Ramsay would *always* be presiding over the boeuf-en-daube, the darkness outside lapping at the windows. Here shall John always stumble; there shall Jane's heart always break.

top. Worry about his inability to get food into his mouth except by slapping his entire open hand on a highchair tray full of Cheerios and eating the ones that stick to his palm. Ask yourself why the other children at his preschool seem so brilliant: they talk, they play together, they daintily fish small objects out of bowls and boxes using thumb and forefinger with surgical precision. They scribble with crayons. They are industrious, productive, dramatic, acquisitive, opinionated, and attention-seeking. They put wooden beads on a string and stack blocks and lay plastic barnyard animals on the plastic barnyard floor for a nap. They seem interested in what others are eating and bring incredibly sophisticated lunches—pasta in Rubbermaid containers, orange sections, even sushi. Ask your son's preschool teacher why he's so different from the other kids. When she tells you to stop being competitive Silicon Valley parents and urges you to recognize that every child is different, make a half-hearted joke about how Jordan would probably starve to death unless he fell face-first into a bowl of Cheerios. Laugh, but not really. Avoid making dinner. Get take-out Chinese.

Engage in circuitous conversation with your husband, who is in his third year of a psychiatry residency, while picking at the BBQ pork chow fun. Hypothesize that Jordan is working on his gross motor skills (mostly running and climbing), which must be why his social skills and language development are lagging. Ascribe his repetitive habit of opening and closing doors (which friends and relatives are starting to notice) to his testing out of cause and effect. Attribute his lack of meaningful speech (mostly nouns, and an unsettling tendency to repeat snatches of conversation and things he hears on TV) to the fact that he's hearing two languages at the same time. Stop speaking Russian to him. Leave most of the chow fun on your plate. Ask your pediatrician why Jordan doesn't call you "mama" or your husband "daddy" and scribble "check hearing by three y.o." in your day planner. Drink more coffee.

Stand in the tiny kitchen of your rental while your husband comes home one afternoon and opens a hefty tome of the *Diagnostic and Statistical Manual of Psychiatry*, 4th ed. on the breakfast bar. He's been doing a rotation through the Pervasive Developmental Disorders Unit at Stanford and has to dress up for work. He's only twenty-eight, and in his shirt and tie he looks impossibly young, like a teenager playing dress-up. Lean over the page marked "Pervasive Developmental Disorders and Autism" so when he says, "I think I know what's wrong with Jordan," you can follow his finger. Experience a stomach-punching pang of recognition as your eyes run down the diagnostic criteria.

When you meet his eyes over the book, you will know: your life is about to change irrevocably.

No cooking that night. Just bowls of cereal on the couch, only because you have to eat something, as your husband tells you he made an appointment to have Jordan evaluated at Stanford. Because he is house staff, you will only have to wait two weeks to learn what, exactly, is wrong with Jordan. How bad it is. As opposed to six months, like everybody else. Remember: you are not like everybody else.

2.

Go for the evaluation. It's a two-day process: on the first day, they test Jordan and watch him not play behind a one-way mirror. Wince when he doesn't respond to his name; when the examiner calls him with feigned cheerfulness to roll a ball back and forth. Feel a little glimmer of hope when he touches the red rectangle in response to the oddly telegraphic prompt, "touch red." Whisper to your husband "That's good, right?" and watch him nod imperceptibly, his eyes far away.

Come in without Jordan on the second day. Sit with the child psychiatrist in a sunny room and answer dozens of questions about your pregnancy, Jordan's birth, family history of mental illness. Force a laugh when the psychiatrist remarks on how socially adept you and your husband seem to be. Try not to let your voice break when you ask whether Jordan is ever going to know—or care—that you're his parents, whether he'll love you, whether he'll be capable of hugging you spontaneously, without one of you holding his hands behind the back of the other.

Be careful when you ask about prognosis and what to do next. Don't think about how precarious life will be for a child with special needs, how much harder. Don't think that you are in way, way over your head. Don't think about how clueless you felt when you brought Jordan home from the hospital and how that was nothing compared to this. The psychiatrist is recommending years of occupational therapy, speech therapy, and behavioral intervention; try not to panic. Swallow your terror, your grief, your bewilderment as you have swallowed your prenatal vitamins. You have done everything right during pregnancy. You have abstained from coffee, sushi, soft cheeses, red meat. Scream only in your head: this is not not not what you signed up for.

Back home, you haven't eaten since . . . actually, you can't remember when. Grab the first thing you see in the refrigerator, a rind of parmesan with just the tiniest sliver of cheese left for you to gnaw. Use both hands to keep your fingers from shaking. Use your teeth—it's salty and pleasantly rubbery—so you have something to do with your mouth other than howl.

Your mother will bring dinner the next night—roast chicken with sage and fresh bread and potatoes with olive oil and rosemary—and even though you only pick at the food, it makes your duplex smell like home, not like simply a place where bad things happen. Try not to meet her frightened, pleading eyes; pretend not to see your father pacing, pacing, his engineer brain trying to work out a solution; avoid this gnawing thought that you have disappointed them.

3.

Everyone must continue with their daily routine.

Ask Jordan's preschool teachers, who now look at you with a mix of caution and pity, to encourage him to try other foods during snack time, to not let him lie on the floor watching the wheels of the toy trucks he rolls back and forth in front of his face.

Continue teaching part-time in the freshman humanities track at Stanford (you plan to finish out the year, because it's already May anyway, and what good would it do to leave now?) and pretend like nothing is wrong. Try not to draw mental comparisons between your son—who, at almost three, is still not toilet trained, still won't play with toys, still has no meaningful speech, still won't call you "mama" spontaneously—and the vibrant, articulate, opinionated young people in your discussion section who make incisive comments about *Robinson Crusoe* and *Frankenstein* and *To the Lighthouse*, flirt unabashedly with one another, and put on adaptations of David Ives' plays for the dorm talent show. Do not, under any circumstances, imagine what they must have been like as children.

Drop off Jordan in preschool, teach your classes. Hit 2:00 p.m. somehow without eating breakfast or lunch. Go to the coffee house swallowing a sudden sob as you cross the quad when it hits you that your child has autism. That's exactly how it comes to you, like someone knocking on your head with a two-by-four: "My. Child. Has. Autism." Get coffee and a croissant because for some reason it sounds like it would hit the spot. That spot: the one aching under your heart that only goes away for a few hours when you fall asleep and comes right back when you wake up to hear Jordan screeching, which he does every morning upon waking.

Repeat for several weeks. Pass your reflection in the mirror and realize that your collar bones are sticking out alarmingly and that even though you are eating a croissant every day, that's pretty much all you're eating. It does and does not hit the spot.

4.

Keep the brave face on at home. Keep it on at least until your husband says, "It's kind of like grieving, you know? Like all the other parents got on the fun train to Disneyland and we . . . " When he breaks off, cry into his shirt for what feels like hours. Then roughly wipe your face with a kitchen towel and run down to Safeway and buy Haagen-Dazs bars—vanilla dipped in dark chocolate, three to a box, the kind you used to eat with other counselors on hot afternoons at summer camp after the campers went home. Eat one apiece and sloppily share the last. Lick the wooden stick clean. Is there anything sadder than a wooden stick that's been licked clean of ice cream?

5.

Start making a catalog of—it's okay—all the things your son didn't do: babble, coo, snuggle, point out or share objects of interest, imitate you, string words together into sentences. Study what the list reveals. How much you missed.

And because of that, you find yourself discarding your resolve not to have any more children, just like that. You want to feel a baby's head burrowing into the hollow between neck and shoulder, a toddler hand pulling urgently at yours, a child's voice summoning you. It's so hard, this asymmetrical parenting, this almost total lack of reciprocity, and it seems so effortless for other parents. Admit it to yourself. You want another baby.

But first, infrastructure. Read scads of books about behavioral intervention and set up a home program. Buy two small yellow classroom chairs and a classroom table at a nearby school supply store. Teach your son to make eye contact using a Cheerio held at eye-level and give it to him when he looks you in the eye, however briefly. Teach him to label objects around him and string together word combinations. Cheer madly when he succeeds and marvel at how much he is learning, and how quickly, even though it seems to be a totally counterintuitive way to teach a three-year-old to do anything. Alternate moments of gratitude with moments of panic when you realize how much he still does not know, may never know, because there are just not enough minutes in the day to teach him all those things that he is not picking up on his own. Realize you haven't had breakfast and eat half the Cheerios in the reinforcement bowl. Eat most of the olives in the bowl of aversives (it's amazingly easy to teach him to say no instead of screeching by offering him an olive, which he hates, and immediately prompting, "Say no"). Go out for Mexican food and hold a tortilla chip at eye level while he screams and lunges for the chip and you prompt him to say, "Chip, please." Ignore the disapproving looks from the other diners. Try not to stare at the little boy at the next table, about Jordan's age, who is persistently pulling on his father's sleeve saying, "Daddy! Daddy! Hey Daddy! Look what I can do!" while his father acts like that's the most normal thing in the world. Leave most of your enchilada on your plate and get it to go, then throw it away after it sits in the refrigerator, untouched, for a week.

Finish teaching at Stanford and become your son's full-time preschool aide. Encourage him to notice other children, to stay seated during circle time, to try the goldfish crackers at snack time. Sometimes he will approach another child, his head cocked inquisitively, and hold out a toy, and your heart will soar; sometimes you will have visions of him in an institution, opening and closing doors, his head tilted to the side. During naptime, walk across Quarry Road to the mall, get coffee and a croissant, and plan your trip to Italy. You made the reservations in another life before Jordan was diagnosed, and now your parents are insisting you must take the trip anyway. Even though he now comes with a roster of speech therapy and occupational therapy appointments and a home-based behavioral program with exercises and data sheets, they will watch your son.

Sit at the Palo Alto Coffee Roasting Company and make a list of the places you would like to visit in Rome, Florence, Venice, Lucca, Siena, San Gimignano. Whisper the names to yourself like a benediction, picture the narrow, winding street where you lived with your parents when you were nine while waiting for the paperwork that would admit you to the United States. Write "Via Tomasso Campanella," with a question mark.

Drive your son to your parents' house the night before your flight to Rome. Find your mother glued to the television: while you were on the freeway singing along to "Baby Beluga," Princess Diana was in a horrific car crash in a Paris tunnel and is in critical condition. Acknowledge the world turning on a dime, like that: TV with your mom; sunny-side up eggs your dad makes, their blanket of fresh dill and torn basil leaves, their festive smattering of red pepper flakes; Jordan's body stiffening and pushing back, just imperceptibly, when you try to give him a hug. Tell him to be good for babushka and dedushka. Remember, only later that night after Diana dies of massive injuries, her elaborate wedding dress with that crazy long train.

Fly to Rome. Squeeze your husband's hand on the airplane. Catch a reflection of yourself in the Da Vinci airport plate glass windows and decide that in spite (or because of) your coffee-and-croissant diet, you look pretty darn good. Wander Rome in a jet-lagged daze, taking each other's pictures in front of ornate doorways and on the Spanish Steps and by the entrance to the house where John Keats lived. Check out the twin churches at the Piazza del Poppolo, then run across the piazza, dodging scooters and cars and laughing, and stop in at a small café with snacks behind glass on a street called Via Babuino, whose name makes you inordinately happy for a reason you can't explain. Discover sheepishly that a fruit salad is not called *insalata di frutta* but a *macedonia* and it's the best thing you ever tasted. At dinner, order house-made pasta with a porcini sauce so indecently rich it pulls an involuntary moan from your throat. Find a café in Florence down the street from the converted fifteenth-century monastery that is your hotel, where the cheerful, plump woman at the bar recognizes you on your second visit and trills "*Buongiorno! Un cappuccino e un té!*" and puts your order on the counter together with two warm *cornetti* fresh from the oven.

Although the Leaning Tower of Pisa is overrated (that's what you decide, anyway), take the obligatory picture of your husband in the foreground pretending to prop it up, then have him take one of you. Propping up: that's what you've been doing, and it's hard, but this is just for fun. In Florence, visit all the places described in *A Room with a View*, the movie you saw on your second date with your husband when you were both seventeen: Santa Croce, Dante's tomb, the Giotto frescoes, Piazza della Signoria with its harsh, stony grandeur; that fountain, those statues, so much naked flesh, violence, lust. In Rome, visit a crypt where generations of monks' bones are arranged in intricate patterns. Eat gelato at least twice a day, whether you need to or not. In Venice, devour squid ink pasta and, at breakfast, copy the clever way the Australian couple at the table next to yours eat their kiwi fruit. At the Piazza San Marco, discover that pigeons have unexpectedly warm, prehensile feet when they perch on your forearms to peck at bread crumbs. Go to the place described in *Cheap Eats in Italy* as having the best sandwich in the world—paper-thin slices of bresaola, parmigiano-reggiano, arugula, a splash of olive oil, and a drizzle of lemon juice pressed between still-hot slices of pizza bianca— prepared by elderly men in dirty white undershirts.

Suddenly, you are hungry for it all.

Because you and your husband haven't touched, really touched, each other in months, rediscovering each other's hands, lips, bodies will feel like a wound knitting together. In Venice, in a hotel room decorated in the palest shades of gray, translucent light coming in off the water in the canal, you will feel unmoored and floating free of everything. In Florence, you will find each other on sweaty, fevered afternoons when you ostensibly return to your hotel room for a nap. Fall asleep holding hands.

And then, in spite of all your misgivings, feel something else: this missing of Jordan even if you suspect he doesn't even know you are gone. Though it will turn out that he does: your parents will bring him to meet you at the airport—impossibly older-looking, shaggy-haired, already growing out of the T-shirt that fit him when you left—and his face will light up when he sees you. He will lunge toward you out of your mother's arms and yell, "Mommy! Daddy!" unprompted. Unprompted is a huge deal; usually, he needs to be prompted to look, to respond, to react, and your heart swells at this unfamiliar spontaneity. And though he will stiffen when you move to hug him, you hold on to that lunge, that "Mommy! Daddy" just like you'll hold on to the feeling of pigeon feet on your arm—a wild thing, momentarily brought close.

And when the two parallel lines appear in the window of the pregnancy test three weeks later, another feeling, or a feeling that is the lack of a feeling: no surprise. For you figured there was a reason you had been feeling fuller.

▶ What does it mean to you to be educated?

—GEORGETOWN UNIVERSITY

Frankenstein is a book about what happens when a man tries to make a baby without a woman. That's what I tell my students when I'm six months pregnant, and though they dart furtive glances at my expanding bump, no one says anything while we discuss Mary Shelley's long history of miscarriages, stillbirths, and deceased children. And while I haven't articulated it to myself, like Victor Frankenstein, I want it all: an academic career, a baby, a child whose disability my husband and I will bravely confront and vanquish. We've bought a house in Palo Alto, the place where everyone has to be good at something, and that's what I'm going to be good at: being the woman who can do it all.

In one of my seminars, two students get into an argument about what it means to be a good person. One of them brings up Aristotle's claim that virtue is acquired, not innate, that it's nothing more than the mechanical repetition of virtuous acts—which means that anyone can change. The other student, a boy with perpetually disheveled hair and wire-rimmed glasses that slide down his nose as he gesticulates, argues that it's impossible, that people are either intrinsically good or intrinsically bad, and no amount of repeating good actions can change a person's true nature. His opponent, who is knitting a heather-blue scarf as she sits cross-legged in her chair, clicks her needles as she skillfully parries his arguments, and I try to suppress a smile because I am totally on Team Aristotle.

For what is applied behavioral intervention, ABA for short, if not the mechanical repetition of virtuous acts? It breaks any task, no matter how complex, into small, manageable steps, rewarding the successful completion of each step, and, through mind-numbing repetition, chains those steps together into increasingly sophisticated behaviors. David and I have found Jordan a nursery school aide, a sunny, kind, patient student at a local community college who trails him throughout the day and gently points out what in behavioral intervention terms is called "social opportunities" and in lay terms, "splashing at the sensory table" or "sitting with everyone else for snack time." So successful is this virtuous repetition that in less than a year, Jordan has learned to dress himself, speak in sentences, and we are right now, this very moment, working on emotions. "Make a sad face," we say; "Make an angry face"; "Make a happy face." Almost all of Jordan's faces look surprised, but he really tries, and when he makes an angry face that entails raising his eyebrows while screwing up his mouth and emitting a convincing growl, we all laugh.

None of this is natural, but it seems to be working. Jordan is not unhappy—if anything, he seems happier, more connected, more industrious, more . . . normal. He no longer screeches when he wakes up in the morning. We tell ourselves that behavioral intervention will give him options: to verbalize what he needs, to connect with others, to live an independent life. We reassure ourselves by quoting Temple Grandin, an animal scientist diagnosed with severe autism as a toddler, who ascribes her success to this kind of teaching.

Still, we have misgivings; we ask ourselves, and each other, if pushing Jordan this way is the right thing to do. We are not—*not*—like Victor Frankenstein, and Jordan is not our creature, but we can't help but feel that we're somehow violating the natural order, disturbing with profane fingers what shouldn't be disturbed. Who are we to decide what is normal and to decree that normal is what Jordan should be? Yes, in eight months he's gained two years on the Denver Developmental Scales (the chart is in the middle of our refrigerator door, next to Jordan's scribbled drawings in which we've counted how many body parts his people have (the more the better, according to the Denver)), but is that how we're supposed to measure progress?

After we put Jordan to bed, we obsess over the chances of having another child with developmental delays. Because we already have a child with autism, our chances to have another one are higher—potentially as high as 10 percent. We convince each other that we can do this again if we had to, but we also want, desperately, a neurotypical child. "Look," David says, "If you knew you had a 90 percent chance of winning the lottery, you'd play, right?" I agree, yes, I would. Anyway, we're already playing. We've bought the ticket and everything.

▶ Villanovans are known for "holding doors open" because inclusion is at the core of who we are. Take us on a journey through your background and describe how your life experience has shaped your understanding of the word "inclusion."

—VILLANOVA

I saw a bird at the top of the tree
These were the words he was singing to me
God loves us all in a wonderful way
Be happy, be happy, be happy today.

—preschool song

"Indistinguishable" is the holy grail for parents of high-functioning autistic kids. It's a term that suggests that given enough support and training, a child with a serious neurological impairment could fly under the radar in complex social situations—school, summer camp, the grocery store—with minimal assistance from parents or teachers or others in the know. It's what parents of neurotypical children take for granted and what for many parents of autistic kids (or me and David, anyway) represents the loftiest pinnacle of accomplishment. To help us summit that particular Everest, Jordan's preschool teachers would have to be willing—and able—to subtly redirect his eccentric impulses and help him blend in, to help him connect with other children, to hold high expectations while swaddling him in protective layers of affection, all without drawing undue attention to the fact that he is somehow different. They would combine the relentless good cheer of Mary Poppins, the indefatigable patience of Anne Sullivan, and the no-nonsense toughness of LouAnne Johnson from *Dangerous Minds*.

Needless to say, I quickly come to doubt those people existed.

I call dozens of schools, most of which politely decline my request for a visit to see if their preschool program might be the right fit. The rejections are devastating, though in retrospect, I'm not sure why it surprises me that most people find the prospect of admitting a preschooler with a developmental delay and an entourage of aides (including his father and heavily pregnant mother) who would take turns facilitating his social interactions unappealing. But each rejection—"He sounds exceptional, but I'm so sorry—we're just not set up to be able to help a child like Jordan"; "We would love to help, but it doesn't seem like he would be a good fit for our program"—feels like a stab to the heart. We don't want your kid, they seem to be saying. Put him in special ed, where he so clearly belongs.

After several weeks of fruitless searching, I find Sequoia Preschool. The good news is that they're willing to take Jordan. The bad news is that they lease space from a church.

My troubled history with the intersection of education and religion goes way back, beginning with my arrival in the fourth-grade classroom of a Jewish elementary school right around Passover, a holiday that celebrates the successful flight of persecuted Hebrew slaves from a hostile land ruled by a vengeful pharaoh. My father in a suede jacket with wide lapels, my mother in a turtleneck, me sweating in a sheepskin coat with a fur-trimmed hood—what were we if not modern-day Hebrews, newly arrived in the Golden State from a hostile land with the Hebrew Immigrant Aid Society coming before us like a pillar of fire? Granted, we were modern-day Hebrews who knew not the customs of the land to which they have been summarily delivered—okay, doubly ignorant modern-day Hebrews, bewildered by English words and concepts (cookie, insurance, carpool, take it easy), words that wrenched our Russian tongues and our Soviet brains, and even more stymied by unfamiliar Hebrew words: *haggadah*, *seder*, *charoset*. We didn't know from Passover; my parents had no idea that anything with leavened flour was strictly forbidden during the eight days of its observance, and I caused a near-scandal by bringing a roll to school for lunch.

For the first three years in the United States, we bought a Christmas tree in accordance with the Soviet custom of putting up and decorating a New Year's tree on December 31, while our neighbors wondered what the hell we were doing and what kind of crazy people went Christmas tree shopping on December 26 (people who enjoy a good bargain, that's who). When I was twelve, we moved from San Francisco to Sunnyvale, a suburban town in the heart of Silicon Valley, and there, on the advice of their Irish Catholic neighbors, my parents placed me in St. Lawrence Academy (whose headmaster assured us that students of all creeds and religions were welcome, but only, as I came to suspect, so that the Catholic kids could torture them, like a feeding-Christians-to-the-lions-in-the-waning-days-of-the-Roman-Empire-type situation, only reversed). In the compulsory religion class, where Sister Veronica, a gaunt and terrifying nun, promised eternal damnation for all those who don't accept Jesus in their heart, everyone snuck looks at me; at Mass on the first Friday of each month, everyone around me knelt while I remained seated, lined up to receive communion while I remained seated, and lined up to go to confession while I remained seated. And then, to make it worse, that same year my parents joined Temple Beth Am, a contemporary, glass-walled, reform synagogue on a hill in nearby Los Altos Hills, and signed me up for Sunday School classes that would, in theory, lead to my becoming a bat mitzvah. After two months at Beth Am, I declared to my parents that I was done with Sunday school, that the kids were snobby and mean and the classes boring.[16] This was true, but it is equally true that it's as difficult to find your place at a Jewish Sunday school while attending a Catholic junior high as it is to find your place at a Catholic junior high as a Russian-Jewish émigré. Perhaps I wasn't looking in the right places, but none of these were my people.

When David and I got married, we got along so well because we were both sarcastic and skeptical and irreverent in almost exactly the same way and because neither one of us had any particular use for organized religion. David is an atheist, which scares me a little bit, not because I believe in god, but because I prefer to reserve absolute judgment, just in case. Otherwise, our priorities are identical. We both love the ceremony and the ritual and the stories—the hush that falls over the table when we light Shabbat candles, the clear, pure symbolism of the Seder plate, where everything is part of a narrative thread stretching back thousands of years—but we don't want to attend services, or keep kosher, or join a temple. We worship at different altars: at bookshelves overflowing with meticulously annotated Norton editions of literary classics, at David's complete collection of the writings of Stephen Jay Gould, at lectures and museums and classical music concerts. We hold achievement and curiosity and hard work and creativity as the holiest of holies, and so

16. Only later would I come to appreciate the beautiful irony of the fact that one of those kids—who wasn't mean at all, just quiet and unobtrusive—would become my husband.

when Jordan is diagnosed with autism, we do not rail against a higher being or pray for a miraculous cure or bargain. We set out to help him the only way we knew how: through focused, diligent, scientifically validated effort. (And okay, yes, we worship at the altar of the Denver Scales, where we track whether Jordan can identify colors, use sentences with more than five words, dress himself, and imitate an action.) This is why the irony of finding Jordan a preschool housed in a church is not lost on me.

Sequoia Preschool is in Redwood City, off Jefferson Avenue, past the Cavalry Second Baptist Church, where a large banner across its facade proclaims that Jesus Christ Is Real and Alive. The church housing Sequoia School has no banners—it's just an inconspicuous whitewashed building in a cul-de-sac with a row of classrooms in an adjacent wing, small enough to be intimate but not stifling. Its six teachers have taught there for years, many of them since their own grown children were preschoolers; it's well-worn, well-loved, and very well-organized. The children are uniformly well-behaved: they sing energetically at circle time and say "please" and "thank you" at snack time as though they really mean it and play with the kind of quiet and purposeful industry that we can only dream of for Jordan. Its teachers seem sympathetic, engaged, and genuinely interested in learning as much as they can about mainstreaming an autistic child into their program.

On my first visit to the school, I speak with the director and explain to her that we're Jewish. Would that be a problem? I don't want Jordan to stick out any more than necessary; he already comes with a lot of baggage. "Oh," Mrs. Glennon, the director, says earnestly, "We don't consider ourselves a religious school. We welcome everyone. We celebrate traditional holidays, but we would love to have Jordan share the holidays you celebrate at home."

David likes the school, but reaction from the rest of my family is mixed. My father says that they'll teach Jordan some discipline; Grandma Ester expresses qualms about placing Jordan in a school where the teachers might tell him that his people killed their Lord. But we go ahead anyway, and in September, Jordan shows up wearing a new navy blue polo shirt and khaki shorts. Mrs. Glennon affixes a name tag with JORDAN in bright block letters and a picture of a smiling teddy bear to his chest, and he is launched.

At Sequoia, we discover women of the type we thought existed only in the novels of Barbara Pym: women who wear makeup only on special occasions, who address each other and all the parents, no matter their age, as Mr. and Mrs., who are unfailingly kind, who own vests representing every season and every holiday—Halloween vests with scarecrows and pumpkins, Thanksgiving vests with plump turkeys, Christmas vests with snowmen and holly branches, St. Patrick's Day vests with leprechauns and shamrocks, Easter vests with flowers and ducks and bunnies. They're cordial and encouraging and seem to have never said a cross word to anyone in their entire lives.

At first, Jordan does not blend seamlessly into Sequoia School. He can't sit still at circle time and has to be restrained from wandering over to touch the keys on the piano Mrs. Lin plays every morning. Picking up his napkin at the conclusion of snack time and throwing it in the trash is an ordeal. He can't for the life of him say the short grace before snack—"Thank you for the food we eat / Thank you for this special treat / Thank you for the birds that sing / Thank you God for everything"—and instead lunges for whatever is on the table, avoiding my restraining hands and cackling maniacally.

But as the months pass, he begins to blossom. David and I still have to prompt him through much of the day, to direct his attention to another child who had spoken to him, to remind him to look at the teacher leading a song and to imitate the hand motions, to glue the eyes on the cardboard bear in the place where the eyes go and not just two random spots. But everyone at Sequoia is tactful and kind. Mrs. Higgins unobtrusively slides next to Jordan as he moves a toy car back and forth on the rug and shows him how to make a racetrack with blocks and enlists two other boys to come and have a race; Mrs. Robertson patiently moves his hands through the appropriate motions during singing time; Mrs. Lin shows him how to climb the tall red metal horse in the yard during recess.

The only time I experience a twinge of misgiving was during the Christmas Sing in the church, when the teachers' faces bloom with clumsily applied, too-pink lipstick and the children, in Dickensian white collars cut out of paper, line up and sing "Baby Jesus, in the manger / I love you!" in clear, angelic voices. Amanda Keller is the Virgin Mary, radiantly blond beneath a blue head cover. She crouches near the altar over a crib holding a toy baby Jesus, and Jordan, who is one of the shepherds, sits nearby clutching a small stuffed lamb, a cloth tied with yarn around his forehead. He stares straight ahead, his eyes fixed like a deer in the headlights, and occasionally moves his lips, although not always in sync with the words.

"Is that Jordan?" Grandma Ester asks loudly, squinting at the stage. "Why is he dressed like an Arab?"

"Shhh!" says my mom.

"Doesn't he look a little dazed?" I whisper to David as he focuses the camera.

"Listen," David hisses back, "dazed is good. Dazed is quiet. He could have taken his clothes off and run screaming around the altar."

Still, there's no denying that Jordan is doing well. Everyone says so: his speech therapist, our behavioral consultant, my and David's parents, all the teachers. It's a miracle: slowly, haltingly, uncertainly, but undeniably, Jordan is being reborn. He gets to the point that we no longer have to accompany him to school every day; he has playdates with a boy named Evan; he brings home art projects—leprechauns with dancing hinged legs held together with paper clips, tissue paper blossoms glued to cherry tree branches—that don't differ all that significantly from those of the other children. Another miracle: our second son, Noah, is born in May, almost a year to the day after Jordan's diagnosis. Jordan is mildly curious and, for the most part, gentle (though at school, he bonds with another student who also has a baby brother, and they take turns depositing a Fisher-Price baby into a dump truck, driving it to a toy garbage can, and dumping the baby out). Noah tolerates being schlepped everywhere in his car seat or carrier with extraordinary equanimity and burrows his head into my neck when I hold him and smiles winningly at everyone who comes within his line of sight, and the relief David and I feel at this extraordinarily unremarkable behavior is enormous.

And then it's June and Sequoia School is preparing its Monday-Wednesday-Friday class for graduation.

So we all sit in the main chapel of the Congregational Church, David and I and our parents and my grandmother and Noah, cooing placidly in his car seat, amid about a hundred and fifty other parents and relatives and friends. Mrs. Lin strikes up "Pomp and Circumstance" on the piano and the children file in. Mrs. Robertson and Mrs. Higgins are seated in the very front on little chairs to help guide the children through the hand motions, and as Jordan walks past them and takes his spot on the masking-tape lines taped to the altar for this very occasion (without pushing or falling over or wandering aimlessly in the wrong direction), I can swear I see both of them wipe at their eyes.

They've taught preschool for over twenty years and have undoubtedly seen children of every stripe, but the sight of Jordan, looking at once ridiculously grown-up and very small in his royal blue graduation robes, still makes them cry. Without question it's for the same reason that David and I sit watching him belt out "I Saw a Bird at the Top of the Tree" with a kind of muted awe: he looks just like everybody else. Not simply because he blends into the sea of royal blue sateen polyester and white pin-on collars but because he *blends in*. He's not giggling; he's not fidgeting; he's not playing with his tassel or even picking his nose like Katie McEachern who, positioned front and center in the first row, is causing her parents untold mortification. He's standing still and looking out at the audience and singing *and* doing the actual hand gestures that go with the song. He even smiles at us shyly a couple of times (after we nearly dislocate our arms waving at him from our seats) and once he waves back, stiffly and awkwardly, but definitely in reciprocity.

These women have spent every Monday and Wednesday and Friday patiently and painstakingly and tactfully walking him through the school day, praising his every effort, capitalizing on every opportunity, seizing and amplifying any remotely social gesture on his part. They're catholic in the original, lower-case sense of the word—all-encompassing and generous and ready to take any child in their arms and press him to their ample flowered bosoms. They believe, exactly as the song says, that God loves us all in a wonderful way, and they follow his example. And even though I hate crying in public and avoid it as much as possible, I take a few surreptitious swipes at my own stinging eyes as Jordan walks over and receives his diploma—his diploma!—and sits back down without tripping or dislodging anyone's mortarboard or otherwise causing a disturbance. Basically, like any other kid.

▶ Tell us about your relationship with a role model or mentor who has been influential in your life. How has their guidance been instrumental to your growth?

—YALE

When Jordan was first diagnosed, my father claimed strenuously that it was David and I who needed psychiatric help, the implication being that we were neurotic parents needlessly concerned over normal developmental variations. At the same time, he claimed that in two weeks' time, with the help of fresh air and strenuous exercise, he could make Jordan good as new. (He now claims he never said any such thing.)

My father may have been wrong about fixing Jordan up in two weeks with fresh air and exercise, but once Jordan begins to make progress in his behavioral intervention program, my father is all in. The program gives Jordan structure, he says. And reinforcement! In fact, it's so effective that all children should be taught that way. (To which my mom puts her hand on his forearm and says, "Marcus, please.")

Getting things done—specifically, getting things fixed—is a big deal for my father. He's a man who can fix anything; after his father died, he apprenticed himself out as an electrician at fourteen, worked as a mechanic and an engineer, owned an impressive tool collection, and never met a broken outlet or loose faucet or clicking car engine he didn't like. But a grandson with a serious neurological disorder—that's outside his wheelhouse. And although ABA helps Jordan acquire core skills—in fact, Jordan is practically an ABA rock star—what it can't teach him is curiosity, initiative, a desire to connect with others. He does however, acquire enough language by the time he's five to label everything around him. Loudly.

"That lady is fat!" he hollers one day at a woman passing us at Target. When I pull him into a side aisle and hiss that this is not a very nice thing to say, he gives me a celestial look and says, "But mom! It's true!"

In the car on the way home, I try to explain the difference between things that are true and neutral ("the sky is blue"), true and nice ("that's a nice shirt!"), and true but mean. Calling the Target lady fat is true but mean. Calling his grandmother "old and sick" to her face is also true but mean. So is yelling "that man has no legs!" at the man in the wheelchair. I know I should be grateful that he's talking at all, let alone talking about things in his immediate environment and not train schedules or mushrooms or fans or whatever else he might have become obsessed with, but like the fisherman's wife in the story, I want more.

And then, right around his sixth birthday, I get more. Jordan develops an obsession with *Star Wars*. To make it worse, a well-meaning friend gives him a battery-operated telescoping lightsaber—the kind that unfurls four feet out from its telescoped position—and he immediately puts it to use terrorizing his two-year-old brother.

"Mom!" Jordan says, while following me around the house, "Was Anakin a kid or a teenager when he joined the Dark Side? Do you become a teenager at thirteen? Do you stop being a teenager at nineteen or twenty? Was Anakin a teenager when he became Darth Vader? Can you be a Sith and a teenager at the same time? How old do you have to be to become a Padawan?" And then he sneaks up behind Noah, and unfurls his lightsaber into Noah's neck, and as Noah screams "Mommmmmm!" in that ear-splitting pitch familiar to aggrieved siblings everywhere, Jordan runs away giggling.

One afternoon, I find him standing in our living room over a wailing Noah, poking the lightsaber at Noah's head, and I lose it. I snatch the lightsaber from his hand and bring it down sharply over my leg, anticipating that it would break cleanly in two. But it doesn't; instead, it bends at an awkward angle with a crack and then goes dark and silent. I throw it on the floor, shout, "We don't hit our brother with lightsabers," grab Noah, and storm out of the room. It's official: we've joined the Dark Side, Jordan and I.

Once my fury subsides, I toss the lightsaber into the garage (for whatever reason, I can't bring myself to throw it away), and there it sits, gathering dust, until my father stumbles across it one afternoon. "And what happened here?" he asks. I tell him the whole story and he shakes his head. Then he asks if he can try to fix it and I say yes.

I don't know how he does it, but after several hours of painstaking labor, he brings the lightsaber back to life. You can still see the white lines in the plastic casing where I bent it, but it again unfurls, and lights up, and makes that awful humming sound. Up to this moment, Jordan has largely ignored my dad, as he does most people unless they get right in his face, and my dad is not a get-in-your face kind of person. And yet, when he proudly and shyly hands Jordan the restored lightsaber, Jordan looks him square in the eye with something resembling awe and says, "Wow. You are really good at fixing stuff."

▶ Solve for x.

—UNIVERSITY OF CHICAGO SUPPLEMENTAL ESSAY PROMPT

I was convinced I was going to have a girl when I became pregnant with Jordan. We had a name picked out: Mara Avery. We knew what she'd be like: dark-haired, dark-eyed, feisty. In the fourth month of my pregnancy, an ultrasound revealed that there would be no Mara. Ditto with pregnancy number two, which resulted in Noah—dark-haired, dark-eyed, affable, charming, but not a girl.

When Noah was eleven months old, David's father unexpectedly died while on a cruise in the Caribbean. He was a big bear of a man with twinkling eyes behind large tortoiseshell glasses who loved popcorn (which he would invariably spill on his chest and belly while eating in front of the TV), Groucho Marx and Pink Panther movies, running, and vanilla ice cream. His death was senseless and entirely avoidable, but because the ship's doctor mistook diverticulitis for indigestion and waited too long before getting him to a hospital, he was gone at fifty-five. David's mother returned alone, hollow-eyed.

Barry has been dead for almost a year when David finds a company in Virginia that uses a centrifuge to separate girl sperm from boy sperm (at least that's how I understand it) and artificially inseminate the chosen gender into the mom. We talk it over and decide to give it a shot in a conversation whose casualness is inversely proportional to the momentousness of the decision and boils down to, "Yeah, this seems like a relatively non-invasive procedure with a high likelihood of a successful outcome, so let's do it."[17] David is still grieving; we're both exhausted and overwhelmed by the demands of raising a six-year-old with special needs and a toddler with regular needs. So why *not* add a third child to the mix? Perhaps more reflection is in order, but we don't feel like reflecting. We don't say this out loud, but what both of us want, I think, is a small corner of our life we can control. Once again my parents tell us they will watch Jordan, and we fly to Washington, DC, with eighteen-month-old Noah.

Noah throws up in my lap during the bumpy landing. In DC, the cherry trees are blooming. So, I would like to believe, are my ovaries—I've been taking Clomid for a month and I'm bloated and emotionally unhinged, one minute ecstatic about the possibility of finally having a girl and the next wringing my hands and demanding hysterically whether people who were raising an autistic child and a toddler should really be using reproductive technology to select the gender of their third child.

The ultrasound before the insemination reveals that in spite of the Clomid, I have not ovulated that month—"Sometimes that happens," says the sympathetic nurse and pats my shoulder—and we return to our hotel, where I sob on the bed and Noah tries to climb on the dresser. The week after we return, David gets a book called *How to Select the Sex*

17. Now that I think about it, this is also how I solved problems in my high school calculus class (when I could be bothered to show up): intuitively, by eyeballing them and deciding on the answer. Mr. Axelrod, who already disliked me, would become positively livid when I would get the correct answer on multiple-choice questions asking to calculate the volume of a revolving solid. "How did you come up with that answer?" he demanded. "It looked right," I would reply.

of Your Child, which explains that having a child of your desired gender was all in the timing. Which, apparently, it is, because the month after we return from DC, I get pregnant.

When the ultrasound shows that our third baby is a girl, we halfheartedly dither over other names—Emily, Emma, Erin—but we already know that she's going to be Mara. Her middle name will be Bryn, in Barry's memory. She's exactly what we imagined: dark-haired, dark-eyed, feisty. She screams without taking a break for four hours on the dot, from 3:00 to 7:00 p.m., until she's four months old. Three months later, she is waving good-bye, pointing, and naming things. Her favorite phrase is "Do it by self."

She and I read all the Junie B. Jones books, *The Witch Family*, *Jane Eyre*. She is fearless: after learning to ride a bike at three, she face-plants and knocks loose her front tooth, which deters her not in the slightest. My friend Nanci gets her a BMX helmet to protect her remaining teeth, and she zooms around our neighborhood on her pink bike with white streamers, wearing what looks like a blue motorcycle helmet and thus earning a great deal of admiration from Jordan and Noah's friends. In elementary school, she starts writing and illustrating her own books. One is about a family of wolves; another, about an intrepid cat named Tom. After our cat Gabby dies, she writes and illustrates a ten-page book: Gabby sleeping on an old wicker bag in the garage, Gabby meowing in the morning, Gabby stalking birds in our yard, Gabby curled up on David's lap. Her kindergarten teacher, eyes crinkling with pleasure, tells us the only problem with Mara is "sneaky reading"—that is, Mara sneaks books from the nearby bookshelves during circle time.

There are times, and this was one of them, when x solves for itself.

▶ How did you spend the last two summers?

—STANFORD UNIVERSITY SUPPLEMENTAL ESSAY PROMPT

By the time Mara is five, David and I begin to believe that we successfully willed into being the charmed life we envisioned for ourselves. Mara is curious and funny and affectionate; Noah acts like the mayor of his elementary school, where he seems to know and like everyone and where everyone seems to know and like him. We discover a family camp in the Sierras and return there for a blissful week every summer. Jordan has friends with whom he tosses a football after school and friends David stealthily helps him cultivate by running elaborate Lord of the Rings-themed games every Saturday. Our garage is full of laminated topographical maps of Middle Earth and boxes of Lord of the Rings miniature figures, which range from a minuscule squatting Gollum to towering Ents. On Saturdays, our house is filled with boys rolling multi-sided dice and yelling about critical rolls. There's dropped popcorn all over the floor. We order pizza and act like this is all totally normal, like we've been the fun house since time immemorial.

We join our neighborhood swim club, and while Noah and Mara play with their friends on the large lawn, Jordan—who at age ten can barely dog-paddle across the deep end—declares that he wants to be on the summer league swim team. The swim team coach and club manager, a grizzled, irascible woman in her sixties named Sue, squints at him and says he can start practicing with the six-year-olds. To our surprise, Jordan acquiesces. Fortunately, he's small, so he doesn't stand out too much in practice. At the first swim meet, he flails down the length of the pool, taking over a minute to swim fifty yards of freestyle while other parents fret over their kids' personal best times and whether they're good enough to be seeded in the top three in their age group. These kids have had years of swim lessons, and we feel like we're behind yet again, so we sign Jordan up for swim lessons with Sue. Sue doesn't suffer fools gladly (she particularly delights in putting hyper-competitive parents in their place), but she takes a liking to Jordan. Jordan keeps coming to practice and staying for hours to practice his racing dive and master the flip turn. At the Champs Meet at the end of the season, he dives in at the buzzer like he was born to it and swims a fifty free in 32.7 seconds, coming in first in his heat. We cheer like crazy, and at the celebratory dinner that night, Sue gives him a coach award for tenacity, humility, and improvement, and we whoop and applaud again like we're the luckiest people in the world.

▶ Describe how you have taken advantage of a significant educational opportunity or worked to overcome an educational barrier you have faced.

—UNIVERSITY OF CALIFORNIA PERSONAL INSIGHT QUESTION

I end up in admission because one of my fellow lecturers at Stanford is also a senior admission director and it becomes a standing joke among the lecturers to needle him about certain students at staff meetings. Like the student who has not said two words in discussion and whose papers, even those on the *Bhagavad Gita* or Dante's *Inferno* or Tolstoy's "The Death of Ivan Ilyich," invariably turn to Baruch Spinoza. Or the one who accuses me of unfairly nitpicking because I circle "for all intensive purposes" on his paper. Or the one who stops a discussion section cold when she asks, loudly and angrily, why great literature has to be so depressing. Jon bristles, carries on about the impossibility of predicting what a student might be like once they materialize in the flesh, and tells us that in spite of the imprecision and difficulty of it all, reading applications and shaping an incoming class is immensely rewarding. Try it if you don't believe me, he says, and looks straight at me when he says it, and I'm flattered and intrigued. It's exactly like being invited to sit with the cool kids in middle school. Plus I can work mostly from home instead of spending my entire teaching salary on daycare. Plus I'm already a Stanford lecturer, so there isn't even an interview process. I am, simply, in.[18] Only later do I wonder if there was something ominous about the dispatch with which the transition from teaching to admission happened, whether the momentum that drove me into the admission office was akin to the inauspicious momentum that drove Agamemnon home to Argos from Troy, Clytemnestra waiting in the palace with bath drawn and dagger ready.

In 1999, the Office of Undergraduate Admission, located in the Old Union, was a heady place. To get there, you walk through a palm-lined courtyard, go up creaky stairs, and follow the signs in a hallway with a red linoleum floor. A cavernous room marked "Credentials" holds the paper files of every single applicant for that season; people who work in Creds are responsible for collating students' transcripts, test score reports, teacher letters of recommendation, and essays, placing them in color-coded files by geographic region, and supplying each file with a yellow work card on which readers write their summaries and recommendations. Down the hall is the Office of Undergraduate Admission proper—a warren of offices and cubicles, fronted by a desk where Mireille, an unflappable woman with a hawkish profile and piercing black eyes and a heavy French accent, answers the phone. The air smells like dust, old masonry, paper, and power.

The Admission Office is scrupulously organized. People who work there walk briskly and talk quietly and say purposeful-sounding things like "decide and commit." The reading process is regimented and orderly. Every Wednesday, we pick up files for the week and meet to discuss the files we

18. Which is kind of funny, considering that I was rejected from Stanford as an undergrad and then, when I applied to the graduate program in comparative literature, was waitlisted and then rejected. But whatever.

reviewed the week before. Files are divided by region; my files are purple and green and include parts of Texas, parts of Connecticut, a large swath of Southern California, and occasionally local schools that are the dean's purview but need a second (or a third, or a fourth) read. At some point, I stop calling students "students" or "applicants" and like everyone else, begin to call them "files." A colleague jokes that a former dean used to call them "my little flat friends."

The work card at the front of each file is pre-printed on heavy yellow stock, with a section for the first reader responsible for the initial sort in which applications are divided into competitive and non-competitive piles. NC: anyone with more than two B's, SAT section scores below 700, a disciplinary infraction, or unremarkable extracurricular activities. Sure, there are the occasional exceptions: a first-generation student, an English-language learner, a student who had been suspended because she organized a student walkout to protest a patently unfair school policy; the student might not have extracurricular activities because he worked full-time to support his family while also attending school. But for the most part, the initial sort is straightforward, and about 65 percent of the applicants, an "NC" for non-competitive circled at the top of their work card, exited the application process. The C's—about 30 percent of them—continue on. About 5 percent of the applicants fall into a third category called "clear admit"—a category reserved for students so exceptional (like, graduate-student level, Olympic-hopeful, Nobel-prize-candidate exceptional) that they float to the top of the pile. The senior deans can reverse the recommendation, but the clear admit designation is a big deal, not to be taken lightly. Weeks can go by without a clear admit, and during other weeks they cluster and shine like jewels in a shipwreck.

The competitive files are the hardest. The year I start reading at Stanford, the university has an admit rate of 12.5

percent. For every ten competitive files I read—competitive meaning that any one of them could potentially be admitted—I have to deny seven of them, no matter what. The remaining three are "swims," which means the application continues to committee but has at least a 50 percent chance of being denied later in the process.

Then the second-round read: a comprehensive evaluation of the competitive students. A full read plus the write-up is meant to take twenty minutes. In my first year, the reading and write-ups take me at least twice that time. In addition to reviewing the transcript and reworking the student's GPA onto a standardized scale, we compare self-reported and official test scores, read through the counselor's letter, the two teacher letters of recommendation, and often, an optional letter of reference from someone outside the classroom. Then we review the extracurricular activities, and then we read the essays. And then comes the hardest part: in a space no bigger than 2" × 4", we sum up the application and our reasoning for the decision—deny or swim.

There are acronyms to circle and boxes to check and shorthand to capture the sum total of a student's candidacy in a handful of letters. ("I will show you fear in a handful of dust," wrote T. S. Eliot.) SSR: secondary school report; TR1 and TR2: teacher letters of recommendation; ORF: optional letter of reference. Reasons for swimming an applicant can include "RIC," which means rank in class, "PQs," which stands for personal qualities, or "glue," which means the student is a connector, a force for good in their community. Reasons for denial can be "ngb" (nice guy/gal, but . . .), "lmo" (like many others); or "dso" (doesn't stand out). The student information section (or SIF) where students list their activities and write their essays might be described with a plus or a minus or with an arrow pointing up or down; a reader might comment on "distance traveled," which means that as a senior, the student has come a long way from freshman year. The SSR, which contains the counselor letter, might be stronger and more substantive than the teacher letters; in admissions shorthand, the observation might look like this: "SSR > TRs." Or the reader might note that a student is a "leg." (for legacy) but has low IV (intellectual vitality) but a high GPA and exceptional talent as a soccer player, though is not a recruited athlete, and utterly unmemorable essays, and if that reader is me in my first year of reading, she will stay up until two in the morning trying to figure out how to distill all that into a 2" × 4" rectangle and vacillate over whether to swim the unmemorable legacy soccer player or the girl with two B's who wrote a brilliant essay about feeling the energy pouring from paintings in a museum, whose teacher writes that he has never encountered a student so curious and so alive.

I learn the lingo and get faster, more precise in my appraisal of each student. Each application is a new world; students from happy two-parent homes, from enormous wealth, from families riven by divorce, by violence, by illness, by addiction, by unemployment, by siblings with special needs (I hold my breath when I read those essays). I discover that I'm biased against students who list Ayn Rand as their favorite author—their applications tend to be dry, pragmatic, unemotional—and have to remind myself to read objectively. I start keeping a list of books I want to read because of the fervor with which students describe them (no one ever describes an Ayn Rand book with fervor). I marvel at students who play multiple varsity sports, who participate in Math Olympiads, who invent things, who dance, who paint, who do those things while working through learning disabilities, autoimmune disorders, blindness. I feel an enormous sense of responsibility to all of them—I want them to be understood, I want the effort they put into distilling their life into five pages of the application to be somehow acknowledged. In my first year, a colleague reminds me that I'm letting them into Stanford, not into heaven, and if they don't get into Stanford, they'll go somewhere else equally good—like Berkeley, she says, her eyes twinkling.

From November through March, reading applications becomes all-consuming. I carry them with me in a tote bag and read in a corner of a coffee shop after dropping Noah off in his morning preschool class. I read them while waiting with Grandma Ester for a prescription to be filled at the Palo Alto Medical Foundation. I read them while I'm pregnant with Mara. After she's born, I read them late at night after David and I settle everyone down, after we read *Mr. Putter and Tabby Feed the Fish* and *Alligator Baby*, and I wonder, not for the first or last time, if Mr. Putter and his elderly neighbor, Mrs. Teaberry, have a thing going or (because I miss academia) whether an academic paper can be squeezed out of Robert Munsch's stories about bright capable children and their inept parents—something like "You've Got the Wrong Baby!: Crisis of Parental Authority in the Works of Robert Munsch." Then David goes to bed, and I'm the only one up, and the house is quiet except for the rustling of paper, nothing but blackness outside our large single-pane windows. To keep down my anxiety over deciding wrong or writing the wrong things on the work card, I eat popcorn. During the reading season, I go through a Costco-sized container of popcorn kernels a week. It's healthier than smoking, and keeping my jaw moving takes my mind off the fact that I'm deciding a student's future, even though I know that the decision really isn't all that momentous—it just feels like it is.

There is such an infinite variety of accomplishment, striving, and resilience that reading applications sometimes feels like drinking excellence through a fire hose. Students who hold patents; who teach dance to blind children; who work the evening shift in the family restaurant seven nights a week; who, despite taunting, proudly wear their hijab, their turban, their star of David, their Dickies pants to prom, their hair short, their hair long. Students who come out as gay; who train themselves to speak through a stutter; who raise llamas, who fly a prop plane to their high school, which is over a hundred miles of Alaskan tundra away from their house; who translate for their Spanish-speaking grandfather at the doctor's office because no one else in the family can; who sit alone in church. A student who (gently, respectfully) steered his falling-down drunk mother home from back-to-school night and was essentially raising his younger siblings while running cross-country and maintaining a 4.0 GPA. (He didn't actually write about any of that; his counselor did.) They have straight A's, university-level courses, test scores in the 99th percentile, teachers who think they're extraordinary. The vast majority of them (87.6 percent the year I first started reading at Stanford, 95.4 percent according to the most recent published figures) will not be admitted.

By my second year in the admission office, I graduate up to conducting general information sessions, where I cover the application review process and conduct a Q&A section at the end. Although I'm a small cog in a big machine, in the general info sessions, I feel like a prime mover, competent and assured and unflappable and wryly funny, a well-groomed gatekeeper to the enchanted land that is Stanford. I perfect a geeky-but-stylish academic wardrobe, with strong Emma Pillsbury from *Glee* vibes: retro pumps with chunky heels, J. Crew cardigans over blouses with Peter Pan collars, calf-length skirts or tailored pants. I put on Lancôme matte cognac lipstick before walking into the room to start the presentation. I learn how to combine an air of knowledgeable authority with clever asides. When the inevitable question about whether it's better to take hard classes and get B's or to take easier classes and get A's comes up during the Q&A, I answer it's better to take hard classes and get A's, turning up a corner of my mouth to suggest that yes, I get it, it's ridiculous. And all the while I know the truth, but can't admit it out loud, no more than I can admit the vast majority of the students in the room to Stanford, and part of me is thinking, *I am so sorry; I know I'm leading you on and giving you false hope*, and another part is thinking, *Get over yourselves, people; there are bigger things to worry about.*

▶ Reflecting on your experience and aspirations, discuss how your life will differ from your parents' lives. Provide concrete evidence to illustrate your position.

—CITY UNIVERSITY OF NEW YORK

After four years of working in admissions, I am haunted by the need, the yearning, the endless rejections. I am cynical and demoralized and the luster is gone. I still feel like I got to sit at the cool kids' table, like I'm doing urgent and important work, like I have my finger on the collective pulse of thousands of high school seniors, but I also find myself second-guessing: What if a student had asked a different teacher for a letter of recommendation? What if she had written an essay about playing mahjong with her grandmother, whom she mentioned briefly in the short answers, and not about her service trip to Mexico? What if her desperation to attend Stanford didn't rise, miasma-like, off the page? Why does the personal essay sing and the shorter essays fall flat? There's no answering these questions and no take-backs—the applications are complete, the decision has been made, the decision is almost always a no—so I return to teaching, but after the charged intensity of admissions work, teaching doesn't feel right either. Meanwhile, friends of friends who had heard I worked in admission at Stanford begin to reach out to ask if I would read their son's essay or give some informal advice to their daughter, and enterprising David suggests I go into college admission consulting and offers to make me a website.

I start to fret almost immediately. In undergraduate admission, private college counselors are anathema: they're considered sellouts, money-grubbing charlatans who capitalize on their admissions experience to provide insider tips—or worse: to manufacture students' applications and essays out of whole cloth. I tell David that admissions consulting is a luxury service, that it's superfluous, that it panders to the rich, that *my* parents would never have been able to afford someone like me (and in all honesty, they probably wouldn't have spent money on someone like me even if they had it to spend), that becoming a college consultant is not why I went to graduate school, and—key point—that I wouldn't be very good at it anyway. David counters that it's an opportunity to teach critical thinking and writing one-on-one and to inject some sanity into an overwhelming process and tells me to stop second-guessing and selling myself short. We're also in the middle of a remodel; the run-down, Formica-countered house with single pane windows we bought in 1999 is in full-blown decrepitude. Behind the kitchen cabinets that we painted a cheerful blue are disintegrating shelves. Drawers rain sawdust on the pots and pans below when we pull them open, and there is a plastic-covered hole in our shower tiles that we haven't had time to fix from when the plumber had to break through to repair a leaky pipe. The stove has two functioning burners left, and one of them works only if you jiggle it aggressively. Noah and Jordan, who share a room, will likely murder each other unless we add a fourth bedroom, and since there's so much wrong with the house already, we're looking at stripping it down to the studs and starting over. Remodel aside, having three kids is expensive; as an independent college counselor, I would make more money than a university lecturer or an admissions reader, a job that—considering how much time and energy it consumes—pays barely more than minimum wage.

The website for Irena Smith Consulting goes live on December 31, 2008. (It doesn't occur to me until a few days in that I missed the prime time for undergraduate applications, which are typically due on November 1 for early action and early decision programs and early January for regular review ones.) But on January 1, I get an email from a student who wants my help with transfer applications, which are due in March, and just like that, I have my first client.

David and I have decided to share his office, which is in a handsome building on Hamilton Avenue in downtown Palo Alto. It's a microcosm of the city: built in the 1970s but styled like a much older Spanish hacienda and full of private equity and venture capital firms, lawyers, psychiatrists, psychologists, and coders straight out of college. A startup on the first floor has pastel-colored spheres hanging in its street-facing window. David works until 3:00 p.m. on Mondays, Wednesdays, and Fridays, and I go into his office as soon as he's done, which is where I meet Robert.

Robert is wiry, self-possessed, deliberate. He wears a button-down shirt and a leather jacket and jeans and Converse high tops and has a high school transcript that starts with all A's, descends into C's and D's his sophomore year, and then soars back to all A's in a transitional program to which he transferred as a senior. He applied to college the year before and was rejected everywhere. He also started a profitable tech company as a middle schooler and is currently working on starting another one. When I ask him about the low grades his sophomore year, he tells me that was the year he'd had gender affirmation surgery. Nonchalantly, he adds,

"I probably should have mentioned that earlier, but school wasn't really on my mind that year, you know?"

I ask more questions. It turns out that his parents, who are first-generation Honduran immigrants, didn't oppose the surgery but also said they wouldn't pay for it, and although most surgeons won't operate on teenagers, he persuaded a surgeon to come out of retirement and paid for the surgery using money he made from the sale of his first company, the one he founded in middle school. He tells me that before the surgery, he had been mercilessly bullied. And no, he didn't write about any of that in his first round of applications. When I ask why, he shrugs and says, "I don't know, really. It seemed like a lot, and I wasn't sure how to talk about it."

The good news is that I have all kinds of ideas about how to talk about it because this is literally what I live for. Robert and I work through four drafts; he's a quick study and responds to my comments and questions thoughtfully and eloquently. I tell him to be as specific as possible, to let concrete details build to larger realizations, and as he describes his experiences, he connects the risk-taking inherent in entrepreneurship with the risks he took in becoming male and reflects on the bigger risk, in his opinion, of remaining female. He asks one of his investors for a letter of recommendation. He writes an additional essay explaining the circumstances behind his catastrophic sophomore year. That spring, Robert is admitted to Haas Business School at Berkeley, Yale, Northwestern, and University of Chicago, and I'm in business.

▶ Susan Sontag, AB'51, wrote that "[s]ilence remains, inescapably, a form of speech." Write about an issue or situation when you remained silent, and explain how silence may speak in ways that you did or did not intend.

—UNIVERSITY OF CHICAGO, SUPPLEMENTAL ESSAY PROMPT

As my practice grows, our home life begins to deteriorate. At least, it feels that way. The division between work and home becomes unbridgeable, a chasm. At work, I wear sharp-toed stiletto heels in neutral tones to convey professionalism and to create the illusion that I am not the size of an average sixth-grader, snug black or charcoal skirts, and fluttery blouses accented with statement necklaces. Students hang on my every word; one family tells me that they now ask each other, "What would Irena do?" when confronted with application-related dilemmas. Then I come home, where I can hear yelling from the driveway, where I'm three inches shorter as soon as I kick off my pumps, where no one listens, where I seethe at David for once again getting takeout instead of teaching the kids how to cook, although being in the kitchen with the three of them is not a fate I would wish on my worst enemy.

In the midst of all this, my mother calls one night, breathless, to tell me she just discovered a TV show called *Sex and the City* and it is so, so, so good and I need to start watching it immediately. I borrow a DVD of the first season from the library and am immediately hooked (although it takes me a day or two to get over the fact that my sixty-year-old mother is now more culturally attuned than I am and how far we've come since our fight about *Lace*). I watch while folding laundry and fantasize about being Carrie Bradshaw, stylish and chic, writing sassy columns while sitting cross-legged on my bed in my underwear. I even buy a long tulle skirt at TJ Maxx, but unlike Carrie, I look like an idiot. No matter: the show is an oasis, and my mother and I spend hours on the phone cooing over the unlikely pairing of Charlotte and Harry Goldenblatt and debating whether Miranda should leave Steve or not.

Meanwhile, Jordan graduates from elementary school, and instead of attending our neighborhood middle school (which has no academic or social support for him), he gets placed in a middle school across town that has a program for students with autism-spectrum disorders. The program is in high demand; it has an application process that includes a parent essay and extensive documentation from Jordan's fifth-grade teacher. What the application doesn't include is Jordan's buy-in; we convince him that the program is the right choice, that he will receive the support and resources he needs to transition successfully to high school, but he's skeptical, and as soon as school starts, it's a hard no. Although he's in mainstream classes three quarters of the school day, he wants to be in mainstream classes all the time. He does not want to be in room C9 learning social skills; he does not want to be associated with classmates he calls "fucking weirdos." C9 is cozy and comfortable with its couches and refrigerator, its Christmas lights twinkling near the ceiling and Tibetan prayer flags strung across the room, but Jordan wants none of it. He wants to be normal.[19]

And there's the rub: while Jordan is not obviously impaired, while normal is close enough to be glimpsed on the horizon, it's still out of reach, and that distance is like a maddening itch he can't scratch—so all his manic energy, all his frustration, all his inarticulate rage goes into making everyone around him miserable and proving that being in C9 is not, as we say in the college admissions business, the right fit. And here he succeeds beyond anyone's wildest expectations.

He begins to throw tantrums and barstools, storms around the house shouting about missing homework (which turns up crumpled at the bottom of his backpack along with decaying sandwiches and broken pencils), and demands to know who stole his chicken (which turns up in the microwave, where he had heated it up and promptly forgot about it). He lies about and denies responsibility for small and large offenses. ("That's good, isn't it? Lying?" my mother asks hopefully. "Aren't autistic kids supposed to be incapable of lying?")

He also develops an astounding ability to sense exactly what would push someone's buttons—a kind of sixth sense one of his teachers calls "twinkling." He follows Mara around, taunting her, until she lashes out or runs in tears to her room. He repeats everything Noah says, either in a monotone or in a British accent, and when Noah explodes, Jordan laughs and runs away. He nearly knocks down another student while riding his bicycle at him full-tilt (he claims that he was going to swerve out of the way at the last minute) and gets suspended. He gets detention for saying, "Look, an inflatable principal!" when Ms. Oliver walks by in a puffy jacket, and although David and I are privately

19. And in the meantime, I spend day after day working with students barely older than Jordan who want to be anything *but* normal—for whom blending in and being like everyone else would be a catastrophe.

amused, the principal, a small, curly-haired woman with a pinched face and a very small mouth, is not. The vice principal, who is in charge of discipline, has my phone number on speed dial; she tries to be encouraging and talks soothingly about learning from mistakes, but we do not learn from mistakes at our house. We repeat them over and over, at higher and higher decibels.

At the end of Jordan's seventh grade year, David and I start talking about a residential program. No one—least of all us—knows what to do with Jordan. Teaching a cheerful toddler how to say yes and no seems ridiculously easy compared to simply coexisting with a mercurial adolescent who is objectively small and slight of build (Jordan doesn't have a growth spurt until high school and even then tops out at barely 5'5") but seems to contain towering reserves of rage. We have tried behavioral charts and social stories and journals and rigid reinforcement schedules and books with titles such as *Your Explosive Child*. We have tried active listening and cooperative limit-setting; we have tried a complicated cocktail of medications; we have taken Jordan to therapists and psychiatrists. None of it helps. Late at night, I enter "what kind of parent sends their autistic kid to boarding school?" into the Google search field, but my search yields only page after page of links to alternative education sites, a Yahoo! answers response beginning with the words "No parent wants to place his child in a residential program . . ." and links to some treatment centers for severely impaired children. Nothing comes up about guilt, anguish, ambivalence, despair, or shame—nothing at all.

The truth is, some parents do want to place their child in a residential program. David and I begin to fantasize about it. Like most fantasies, ours are airbrushed and abstract: we don't know what such a program would look like or what, exactly, it would do for Jordan. All we know is that it would get him the hell out of our house, where he yells and slams doors, David and I yell and force doors open, and Noah and Mara cower under blankets in Mara's bedroom with the door closed. Every wall adjacent to a door handle bears a doorknob-sized hole, half the windows have had to be replaced, and at the end of every day, we wonder whether our neighbors are profoundly deaf or even more profoundly indifferent—or maybe just incredibly tactful—to ignore, for months on end, the sounds of all our breakage.

We go to an educational consultant who charges us hundreds of dollars for a preliminary fact-finding meeting during which we repeat the information we have already provided in detail on the intake forms. Then she tells us that as recently as ten years ago, there were no programs designed to accommodate children with an autism spectrum diagnosis, but now there are several. The problem is that they're expensive and difficult to find. David and I exchange a glance: *And that's why we're here*: *to find them*. She draws a long arrow on a dry-erase board in the corner of the room. "This is the continuum of the educational options available to you and Jordan." She sketches a house at one end of the arrow, the one farthest away from the arrowhead. "The house represents the least intensive intervention, which would be the current home/school situation." Then she draws another house, a few inches closer to the arrowhead. "This would be a local private school designed to accommodate children with cognitive, mental, and learning differences."

"Would that be like Armstrong School in San Mateo?" asks David, who has done his fair share of fact-finding.

"Well," says the consultant, "I hate to jump ahead like that." Then she rattles on about the next step, drawing more houses, one for "typical students looking for a boarding school experience" and one for a therapeutic boarding school designed to treat mental illness and substance abuse issues. "And here"—we've reached the arrowhead at last—"would be a therapeutic boarding school designed to support children specifically with autism-spectrum disorders."

Most of her houses are crooked but not even the most-restrictive-option-house—the "really first-rate" one topping out at $70,000-plus a year—has bars on the windows or a more solid-looking door, though that might help us all clarify what, exactly, we are talking about. My hand itches to add a wisp of smoke curling from a chimney or a tree casting its shade on one of the houses or at least to straighten some of the walls. Appropriate placements, the consultant repeats when she's hit the tip of the arrow, are quite difficult to find. She pins us with a look: Close collaboration will be required. It will not be cheap.

So we make other inquiries—this time informally, talking to people who know other people—which is how we find Redwood Academy, a boarding school in the foothills of the Trinity Alps in Northern California that emphasizes experiential learning and community-building among its students. The parents who recommend it have a son with ASD who is slightly older than Jordan. He attended the school for a year and it transformed him; his parents tell us he learned responsibility and life skills and confidence and returned with new insight about himself and his place in the world. They tell us that the school is run by a family and that everyone—the students, the staff, anyone who has anything to do with it, in fact—is "lovely." "Lovely," the mom repeats. "Really, really lovely people."

I call the next day and spend over an hour on the phone with the intake coordinator, who indeed sounds lovely and also young and so kind that it's all I can do not to cry. She asks incisive questions about Jordan and our family, about what we like and don't like about his current school, details of his diagnosis, and which therapeutic interventions we have already tried. By the time we make an appointment to see the school, which is a five-hour drive from Palo Alto, she seems like an old friend. The appointment is on the day before Jordan is scheduled to finish Stanford Swim Camp, which, mercifully, is a sleep-away camp. We can pick him up after dinner, drive to Redding, spend the night, and then drive the remaining 45 minutes to Redwood Academy, which is located in unincorporated Shasta County, near the town of French Gulch, pop. 100.

On the way to pick up Jordan from swim camp, David enumerates all the benefits of Jordan's five-day absence. We've been able to play board games, read chapter books out loud, hang out by the community center pool, have uninterrupted conversations, and make dinner unpunctuated by frenetic calls for help from the younger two. "See?" David says, "This is what it's going to be like when Jordan's at boarding school." I'm less sure; Jordan had acquiesced to the trip with surprising alacrity, and I'm waiting for the other shoe to drop. "He's going to be a nightmare on the drive up," I tell David. "Or at the school. Plus, how do you even know it's any good? And that they'll take him?"

"Oh, they're taking him," David says. "The Boyds said it was a good school. And I'm not going back with him. So that's that."

"You're going to leave him in the Trinity Alps?" I ask. "Just like that? No change of clothes?"

"Nope," says David. "He's got his stuff from swim camp, doesn't he? We'll ship everything else over later."

"You're kidding, right?" I ask.

"Nope," David says again.

Perhaps his five-day absence had done us all some good, but Jordan seems genuinely happy to see us when we come to pick him up. He helps stow his duffel bag in the trunk, climbs into the back seat without trying to shove me out of the way and sneak in the front, and seems—for the moment, anyway—alert and cheerful and cooperative. He asks what we had done while he was away, who is watching Noah and Mara, whether we will stop along the way or drive non-stop. (We stop along the way, once to get gas and once at a Mini-Mart to buy David some beef jerky, me some coffee, and Jordan some strawberry pop tarts and orange soda.) Jordan is positively charming. He tells us that he learned at swim camp that everyone overcomes challenges, that even Ian Crocker battled depression and Michael Phelps drove drunk, but both of them moved on and won medals and did really well. He sits in the back seat, small and sunburned and animated, his blonde-streaked hair newly cropped, raccoon-like ovals around his eyes from his goggle tan. We talk about swimming and boarding school, why Jordan's great-grandmothers weren't much for swimming or other forms of exercise (as young adults during World War II in Stalinist Russia, they probably had limited opportunities for organized physical activity), and whether eighth grade was going to be much harder than seventh. About an hour south of Redding, Jordan announces with a mix of surprise and pleasure that the ride hasn't been nearly as boring as he thought it might be. "Why is that, do you think?" I ask. Jordan looks thoughtful. "I don't know," he says finally. "Because I talked the whole time?"

The good cheer evaporates when we get to Redding. It's been a relentlessly dry, hot year, and Northern California is engulfed by catastrophic wildfires. A sooty, dirt-gray smoke hangs heavy in the night air and ash drifts down even though the nearest fire is more than forty miles away. Though the hotel room air-conditioning is going full blast when we enter, the smoke has already insinuated itself in our hair and clothes. The room smells like plastic. Our window looks out into the parking lot, so we keep the curtains drawn. It feels like the world is ending, right there, outside our window.

The next morning dawns gray and overcast, and in its dingy light everything seems wrong. I've packed a flouncy top and cargo capris to wear on our school visit, and I look like I'm trying too hard to look young and casual. (Then again, how *does* one dress to visit a therapeutic boarding school that you hope will accept your thirteen-year-old with a temper like an IED?) Jordan flops on his bed, refuses to get dressed, and meets our constructive suggestions with surly rejoinders, among which "shut up" is the most pleasant. We eat breakfast at the Black Bear diner, where my "beautiful arrangement of fruit" turns out to be a bowl of soggy cantaloupe, brown banana slices, and strawberries sitting wanly on a discolored romaine leaf. Jordan orders steak and eggs, the steak smothered under a blanket of white gravy so synthetic it wrinkles. David, who orders the pancake, sausage, and egg combo on the promise to share, does not share. Jordan laboriously cuts up his steak in strained silence.

The bad mood continues on our drive up along the winding curves of Highway 44. Jordan is in the back seat, alternating quiet introspection with increasingly loud protestations: he wants to go home now, this instant; there is no way we are even going to see the stupid school; he doesn't care about any appointment. Then we miss our (unmarked) turn and there's nowhere to turn around for the next four miles and David snaps at me for not finding the right route on the map quickly enough and I snap back that yelling at people while they're trying to read a map is the opposite of helpful.

At the school, we park in front of a rustic cabin with a wooden sign reading "Main Office." Three teenage boys lounging on the front porch look at our car with frank interest. We're ten minutes early in spite of our wrong turn, which is good, since Jordan adamantly refuses to get out of the car.

"I don't give a fuck if people are looking at me!" he snarls. "I'm not going in! And you can't make me!"

The extra ten minutes prove handy for the combination of coaxing, cajoling, and thinly veiled threats that ultimately get Jordan out of the car. He walks stiffly, shoulders hunched, eyes to the ground, into the waiting room, ignoring the boys outside. We go in a pace or two behind—in case, I suppose, he's planning to bolt for the forest.

On our tour of the sprawling campus, we follow dirt paths to the student cabins that rim a large field of dry, trampled grass. We find out that students receive an allowance every week, which increases or decreases based on their behavior, and that they can similarly lose—or earn—privileges based on the same principles. We meet the science teacher, a wiry, enthusiastic young guy with a bushy beard and hair that looks like it's caught the raw end of a bungled experiment. He tells Jordan about weekly paintball games, about white-water rafting, forestry, basketball, and soccer, all of which leaves Jordan cold. As we walk toward the student cabins, Jordan mutters that any school without a pool and a swim team is a sucky school and there's no way, ever, that he's going to go.

The circa-'70s cabins are primitive but clean. Students are allowed to bring their own video game consoles—here Jordan perks up—but they're responsible for monitoring their usage and leaving enough time for chores. All academic work is completed at the end of each class, so there's no homework. Jordan perks up at that as well. The classes are small—so small that students can't hide behind other students or their own goofy behavior. "Everyone in my class is accountable to me and to everyone else and above all to themselves," the science teacher says. We like him. Less so the English teacher, who is wearing too much sparkly gold eyeshadow plastered on her drooping eyelids and who struggles to name a single book in the eighth grade English curriculum. "I like to change them up every year, you know, for variety," she says, running her fingers distractedly through her long hair. Pressed on which books she alternates, she says, "You know, books that talk about the adolescent experience, like the confusion the kids feel. Like, um, maybe *The Catcher in the Rye*?"

At the beginning of the tour, I can't imagine leaving Jordan there. He's so small, and the campus, the looming mountains, the expanse of fields and forest surrounding the school, even the other students, are so big. But as the tour progresses, the school grows on me. Everyone's heart is in the right place, even the English teacher who looks like she might once have dropped too much acid. Yes, the setting is rustic, but couldn't all that nature do Jordan some good? Above all, everything operates in accordance with clearly defined behavioral principles whereby pro-social, positive behavior is rewarded and reinforced by adults who don't necessarily have a personal stake in the lives of the students. No way would his rudeness or resistance evoke the same kind of emotionally pitched, near-hysterical response in his teachers and advisors that it did in us. They would see it for what it was: an isolated instance of disruptive or oppositional behavior, not a harbinger of global failure. A bad day would be a bad day, not a precursor of homelessness or a life of crime or years of intense behavioral therapy going down the drain. He would get to start with a clean slate—heck, maybe he could even last the year without driving these good people crazy and getting sent back. At several points, David and I exchange significant looks, but I can't quite get a read on what he's thinking.

Back in the main cabin, Jordan goes off for his interview with the executive director of the school while we speak with an associate director. We try to keep things light and pleasant, exclaiming over many positives we have seen—clear consequences, small classes, high expectations, beautiful setting.

Larry, the associate director, steers the conversation right back into the deep waters we have been trying to avoid. "Tell me more about Jordan's tantrums," he says. "Is he often violent? How high or low is his tolerance for frustration? What does he typically do when he doesn't get his own way?"

Ellen, the school director, is even tougher. She's tiny, barely over five feet tall, with close-cropped gray hair and striking blue eyes. We meet her after she has spent close to an hour talking to Jordan, and we're both ill at ease when we walk into her office and he walks out, giving us a sideways look. David and I have done things we're not proud of—among them, screamed at Jordan that if he stayed on his current trajectory and kept terrorizing his siblings, he would die alone in the street with no friends and no family—and now we wonder whether our parenting strategies have been disclosed. "Jordan was very forthcoming," Ellen says, her hands neatly folded in her lap, and I know David and I are both thinking, *Oh, shit.*

"You probably know that about him," she continues. "He's very honest about his behavior. He told me he loses his temper easily and that he tantrums." She shoots me a wry smile and adds that according to Jordan, I'm more patient than David, and we both nod. Then she pauses and says, "Look, I've worked with thousands of kids in my career. I've headed a residential center for autistic kids, and I've worked with Asperger's kids, and I've directed an outpatient center for severely emotionally disturbed teenagers and young adults before I founded Redwood Academy. Jordan is really not like any other child I've seen." *Here we go*, I think. *Here we fucking go.*

"I want you to know," she says, "That both of you, and your good opinion, mean a lot to him. He's very proud of what you do and who you are. When I asked him if I forgot to ask him any questions about himself, he said, 'You didn't ask me what my parents do.' He told me you were a college consultant and a college teacher and"—nodding at David—"a psychiatrist. I know it probably doesn't seem that way to you, but he loves you very much."

And suddenly, sitting in her wood-paneled office with its ornate carved furniture, I want more than anything to curl up in my chair and cry and cry and cry about the unfairness and absurdity of it all. How could it be that two adults who loved books and language and *The Princess Bride* and each other would produce a child like this? And so what if he really did love us? Both alternatives were equally horrible: either Ellen is wrong and he doesn't care about us, or she's right and he does but something in his brain makes him utterly incapable of doing anything about it except pissing everyone around him off.

It comes down to this: they won't accept him outright, but they're not flat out turning him down, either. "I think this school could benefit him tremendously and literally help him turn his life around—I really do," Ellen says. "But we have to have his buy-in. As of right now, we don't have that. We could take him on a trial basis, but we can't provide one-on-one staffing to make sure he didn't run off into the forest if he got angry or frustrated or if he antagonized another student and got into a fight with him." Admission is provisional: they'll take him with the understanding that if he proves to be unmanageable within the confines of the school, they will send him back. "And that's not necessarily something you want to burden him with," she tells us. "To get expelled in the middle of the year, to come home, to find that maybe there is no room in his current home school—that would be hard for him, and I suspect he already has some self-esteem issues. He would have to work hard—very, very hard—to make this work, and this is not a kid who likes to be out of his comfort zone." She pauses and adds, with another significant and totally unreadable look, "And he's very, *very* comfortable with you."

So we go home, exhausted. On the drive back, David and I are mostly quiet, and Jordan keeps up a low-level grumble in the backseat about the iPod not doing what he wants and occasionally kicks the back of my seat in frustration and swears, and David yells at him to stop it and threatens to take the iPod away. To distract myself, I think about Jordan's comfort zone. Where is that, exactly? At home with us? In one of the crooked houses on the educational consultant's whiteboard? The cabins at Redwood Academy?

And then there is what Ellen, whose blue eyes seem to have the capacity to lay bare a soul, had gotten out of him in under an hour: that Jordan loves us. It is not a thought that has ever entered my mind.

The I-80 begins a long, gentle descent as it branches off the I-505 and makes its way through Vallejo into the East Bay and toward the Bay Bridge, and as we head downhill at over 80 miles an hour, our conversation heads downhill as well. Jordan voices all his complaints, all his pent-up resolve: he will never suffer that long drive again, he will never go to Redwood Academy where the kids are weird and everything is stupid and dirty and bad.

"Well, something is going to have to change," David roars at him, "because we are not having another year like last year again. And if it means that you have to go away, that's what we'll do." As soon as he says it, we both know, without saying a word, that Jordan is not going away. At least not yet. "Or it could mean you changing your behavior," David adds lamely. *Or us changing ours*, I think.

It's dark when we near the Bay Bridge, San Francisco gleaming across the bay. I'm dead tired, but fighting to keep my eyes open so that if David dozes off I can shriek and alert him to impending danger. My blousy top is wilted from the heat and sticking to me uncomfortably; my flip-flops are filthy. I resolve that if we ever go back to Redwood Academy (we will not), I'll wear walking shorts and hiking boots like everyone else. And a regular T-shirt.

And then there we are, back where we've started, ready to begin another year, another round of tantrums over misplaced socks and stolen chicken and missing assignments. Except now we have the dubious reassurance that Jordan loves us, the one thing granted from the 500-mile trip. Maybe things really will be different this time around; or maybe they have been different all along, other than what we have known.

▶ If you could go back in time, what advice would you offer yourself at the beginning of secondary/high school?

—EMORY UNIVERSITY

Because it says "Stanford admission experience" on my website, and because David is a stone cold genius at Google search optimization terms, the students keep coming. Not just from local schools, but from other states—New York, Texas, Washington, Colorado, Georgia, North Carolina—and then from other countries. I learn from a student who lives in Bangalore that Diwali is strikingly similar to Hanukkah and that the Yiddish word "meh" is apparently universal because it's how she describes her interview with the Georgetown alum. I meet students who live in London, in Dubai, in Ankara, in Islamabad. I learn what a *salwar kameez* is. I learn about Wushu and about a student's grandmother who walked barefoot out of China during the Cultural Revolution.

My students do mind-boggling things: they pull scrap metal out of recycling bins and build fanciful contraptions; they research meth addiction in rural areas; they dabble in molecular gastronomy using homemade tools; they run reading programs at homeless shelters; they read Michel Foucault

(Foucault! I didn't even know who he was until I was a grad student) and form their own theories about systems of surveillance and control. They write novels. They sometimes work in fast-food restaurants—Cold Stone Creamery, Chipotle, Taco Bell—where they learn more in one day than many of their peers in the course of a summer spent in an internship.

I love what I do, but I also begin to feel like I've gotten into a luxury car with leather upholstery and seat warmers and a fancy dashboard display but no brakes, and it keeps going faster and faster and I can't slow it down because I'm the one who put it in motion in the first place. When I started, I envisioned myself helping students mine ostensibly inconsequential moments of their life for meaning, making—like Nabokov's John Shade and Nabokov himself—ornaments out of accidents and possibilities. But as my practice grows beyond juniors and seniors, I'm no longer wanted just for essay help but to help plan students' lives. Parents of freshmen and sophomores, and often middle schoolers, begin contacting me to find out exactly which activities their child should do, what the good internships are, which contests are important to enter and win, what to do over the summer. I refuse the middle schoolers, because I cannot in good conscience sit in a room with a twelve-year-old and discuss college planning, even if my advice comes down to "read a lot and do stuff you love to do," but I take on the freshmen and sophomores, because otherwise I wouldn't be making money between January and June. And because freshmen and sophomores are young, their parents come with them, and I end up working with parents as much as I do with children.

Some parents astonish me with their tact, their kindness, their generosity. They send me flowers and gift baskets. They tell me they're jealous because their children listen to me without question but push back on everything they say. (But not, I think, like my son pushes back on everything *I* say.)

They're humbled by their children's growing independence, burgeoning ideas, and willingness to stretch intellectually. But for others, the application process seems to be a vanity project, as much about themselves as about their child. More, in some cases. I meet a father whose daughter's name is the same as his, with an "a" at the end, and he talks almost the entire time, referring to "our application" and "our approach." One mother, on the verge of tears in a meeting because her son is not doing what she wants him to be doing on a timeline that she wants him to do it on, says that she is not having a positive experience with any of this, at all. They want to make sure we're highlighting what one father calls the "deliverables"—that the application sends the right message. They come to meetings with binders and spreadsheets, which terrify me, because I am the kind of disorganized person who jots notes down on random pieces of paper using a fountain pen, which occasionally leaks, leaving me with a smudge on my cheek where I've rested my hand. I have my intuition and my ability to think on the spot and to synthesize seemingly disparate aspects of a student's life, and they have concrete and unambiguous questions and expectations and demands.

When Noah was a toddler, he'd sometimes come to our bedroom after a bad dream, stand by my side of the bed, and stare intently at me until I woke up. I would jolt upright in bed, heart pounding, until I placed the eyes staring at me from the darkness and reached out to comfort him; now, I feel the same clutching panic—who is that? what do they want?—in the face of the parents' yearning for certainty. They want to be reassured that if their child does X, they will be admitted to college Y, and when I can't provide that reassurance, that clarity, they lash out, either at their child or at me or at both of us. A mother decrees that her daughter's essay in response to Stanford's question about a meaningful learning experience (an essay that the daughter drafted multiple times and agonized over and considered from multiple perspectives) is "not intellectual enough." A father—who happens to be a professional writer—leaves a comment in the conclusion of his daughter's essay, saying it lacks a certain *je ne sais quoi*. Another father blames me for ruining his son's personal statement after his son doesn't get into a single Ivy League school (though he does get into UC Berkeley, with a full scholarship).

Those parents strike me as egotistical, self-absorbed, insane. They sit in my office and tell stories about "all those *other* crazy parents" at their child's school while I fight to keep a straight face because two days earlier, another parent from their child's school sat in exactly the same chair and said exactly the same thing. I see my job as helping students discover who they are in the world and articulate their insights as precisely and authentically as possible, but I quickly come to see that it also includes mediating family conflicts and talking parents off a ledge and managing expectations and trying, diplomatically but firmly, to keep parents from destroying their children. (Or at least I see it as destroying; they see it as helping.) I'm also not unaware of the keen irony of the fact that I'm taking money from people who are trying to get their child into the best college so that I can funnel it into paying for therapists and psychiatrists for *my* child, who, let's face it, is not going to be a contender for Harvard, Yale, Princeton, or Stanford.

Toughest of all are what I privately call "average excellent students"—students with high grades, high test scores, the right roster of extracurricular activities (a varsity sport, robotics, debate, a summer internship arranged through a friend), and no spark. What distinguishes them (or so they, or their parents, think) is their desperate, visceral need to get into Yale, or Stanford, or MIT and to settle for nothing less. When I suggest possible additions to a college list that is so aspirational that it verges on the absurd, a student's mother gives me a scornful look and says, "We're not here for Purdue." I make a ninth-grade boy cry in my office when he tells me he only wants to go to Stanford and will do whatever he needs to do to make that happen and I tell him that while this kind of ambition is admirable, he still might not get in because admission to Stanford is less of a meritocracy and more of a lottery. If, on the other hand, his goal is to get a good education, there are hundreds of other schools to consider. His mother cuts me off and asks, "But what if you're captain of three varsity sports teams?"

"Are you?" I ask the son.

"No," the mother cuts in, "But we could say he is. Who's going to know?" And then to the son, with a sideways look of pure hatred in my direction, "Don't worry, buddy. We'll figure it out."[20]

20. This is our one and only meeting. When they (much to my astonishment) call to schedule a follow-up meeting when their son is a sophomore, I tell them I don't think we'd be a good fit.

▶ Think about an academic subject that inspires you. Describe how you have furthered that interest inside and/or outside of the classroom.

—UNIVERSITY OF CALIFORNIA PERSONAL INSIGHT QUESTION

History repeats itself,
first as tragedy, second as farce.
—Karl Marx, *The Eighteenth Brumaire of Louis Bonaparte*

It's Sunday afternoon in June, 2009. Jordan's Contemporary European History final is tomorrow, and he has a low C and may very well not pass the course. We have just discovered, as a result of quizzing him from a tattered study guide he extracted from the nether depths of his backpack, that he knows almost exactly nothing about contemporary European history, even though he has resisted our overtures to help him the entire semester and claimed he had the subject matter under control. Now he is sitting on the couch in the family room in front of a wrinkled stack of notes and handouts, trying to absorb ninety years of bloody, complicated, heartbreaking, labyrinthine history—two world wars, nationalism, economic collapse, genocide, totalitarianism, the cold war, ideological warfare—for an exam that's scheduled to take place in less than twenty-four hours. I can hear paper rustling. Jordan has already been to the kitchen for a snack and a drink (twice each); he has said provoking things to his brother and sister; he has paced aimlessly back and forth throughout the length of the house. He has covered the study guide with endless doodled cubes and shifted around papers—which are so wrinkled that they won't fit into his folder, which itself looks like it has been masticated by an angry camel—and he has chased the cat around the backyard until David and I yelled at him to knock it off and start studying.

"And then I'm going to do the Nazi party and then the Holocaust and then the Cold War and then I'll be all done," Jordan announces cheerfully to no one in particular from the couch.

All the horrors of the twentieth century and he'll be all done.

During World War II, my paternal grandmother lost her entire family—her parents, her three older sisters, their husbands and children—in an aerial bombardment as they were evacuating Odessa by train. My great-grandparents on my mother's side were shot by advancing German troops in a small town near Minsk and dumped into a mass grave. My grandfather was briefly arrested during one of Stalin's purges. My mother was followed home by two men after we applied to emigrate from the USSR.

I say nothing.

"Mom! Do you think I'm going to fail this class? Will you pay for summer school if I fail the class?"

Silence.

"I'm very bored. This is hard. How am I supposed to know anything about the Holocaust if you never gave me any information?"

Silence. Jordan's restlessness buzzes like a fly in the room. None of this means anything to him. When I was fourteen, a year younger than Jordan is now, my mother had whispered truncated details of what had happened to her mother's family in Dzerzhinsk when the Germans marched through Belarus: old people taken out to the fields and shot, a baby boy literally ripped limb from limb—one soldier grabbed the legs, the other the arms, and pulled—in front of his parents. I could not get the images out of my head for months. If I were to tell Jordan this, he would look at me absently and shrug, as though I had summarized a not particularly interesting video game.

Jordan sighs theatrically. The week before, we had a big blow up about his historical fiction project about the Treaty of Nanking—the one where he situated the action near the Mediterranean Sea in Latin America and we had to pull up a world map on the computer to ascertain that Latin America was, in fact, nowhere near the Mediterranean. Or China. And that it made no sense for the British, who, according to Jordan, "addicted the Chinese to opium," to be hanging out in the Mediterranean, either. The day before, when the magnitude of the problem started looming into view—much like the iceberg that sank the Titanic—he claimed, stridently, that France and Britain faced off in the Cold War and that Britain attacked the United States at Pearl Harbor in 1941. In Canada. Pressed on this point, he shouted, "How am I supposed to know this shit? I've never been to the East Coast!"

I imagine this will all be funny in twenty or so years, assuming that Jordan is not homeless and living in a cardboard box somewhere.

"I'm studying. Right? I'm studying right now, right?"

Silence.

"I'll make you a bet. If I pass this class, you'll give me five hundred bucks. Right? Let's make a bet. Mom! Mom,

I'm talking to you. Do you think I'll pass this class?"

"I don't know," I say.

"I think I'll pass the class. I'm not close, but I'm going to study and I'm going to pass the class. Mom! Mom, are you listening to me?"

"What is there to listen to?" I snap.

"Are we making a bet? We made the bet, right? If I pass, you'll give me five hundred bucks."

I say nothing.

"Can I just have five hundred bucks? Please? I said please. Please is a magic word. Why won't the magic word work? Mom! Mom, I'm talking to you."

Silence. More rustling.

The front door opens and David walks in from a run. "What are you doing?" he says to Jordan.

"Studying," Jordan says.

Then, abruptly, as is always the case, things take a turn. Jordan can't find the answer to a question and peremptorily demands what the first signs of genocide in German hospitals were and what happened to the children. I have no idea which children and which hospitals he's talking about—as usual, Jordan doesn't bother with context and just reads the question verbatim from the very fragmentary study guide—and, after flipping through his history textbook and finding nothing, I tell him to check his notes.

"You do too know the answer," he says. Pause. "You don't even know about your country." Pause. "Jew." His voice rises. "That's just embarrassing. It's a crime is what it is. How can you not know about your own country? You were involved."

At this point, it doesn't take much to send me over the edge. "*What* was I involved in?" I scream, not sure where to start—at his use of the word "Jew" and his blithe ignorance about what such usage implies or his total lack of historical literacy (much like the papers in his backpack, he seems to be lumping all totalitarian regimes into one messy, disorganized pile).

"The Nazi Party," he says.

"The Nazi Party? Really?" Now I have, in the idiom of George W. Bush, gone nuclear. "How old do you think I am? Do you know *anything*?" I pause, trying my best not to call him a moron, which I want to do so badly my teeth ache with the effort of holding the word back. "*You* know nothing about your country!" I yell instead. "Pearl Harbor is not in Canada, for one thing!"

"I know it's not!" he yells back. "It's in Boston! And I can't believe you can't tell me the answer to the question!"

"You want to call me a Jew?" I say. The words come out so hard and fast I can hardly register what I'm saying. "For your information, *you're* a Jew too! And a moron!"

"Shut up!"

"You shut up!"

If I were not so agitated, it would occur to me—as it does much later—that we are re-enacting our own version of twentieth-century European history. In an act of naked aggression, Jordan threatens to hurl his book through the window. To retaliate, David and I make sweeping and ambitious threats: Jordan is going to spend the summer grounded in his room. He will be cleaning bathrooms for the next five years. We will kick him out of the house and he will be sleeping in the gutter. We are going to cancel swim camp. Jordan screams, "Nooooooo!" and tries to tackle David, who grabs the phone and yells, "Go ahead and attack me. I'll call the cops and then I won't have to wait two and a half more years until you're out of the house. They'll take you away right now! This very second!" In ten minutes, we have covered escalation, containment (failed), ideological warfare, and are now teetering on the brink of mutually assured destruction.

Somehow, the threat to call the police—even though we have not yet, thankfully, had to act on it—does the trick. Jordan wilts and retreats to the couch, where the wrinkled notes and handouts await, and where, once again, history is about to repeat itself.[21]

---

21. As a matter of historical record, I would like to note that Jordan passed his final, by the skin of his teeth (like so much else during those years).

▶ What is fairness in the world? Is merit always the pinnacle of fairness in education?

—PENN STATE

My practice keeps growing. From June through December, I work twelve-hour days, including weekends, either editing essays or meeting with students. Emails spawn in my inbox—twelve, thirteen, fourteen—as I speak on the phone in the space of only a few minutes. I hire two editors, Elyse and Laurie, to help with essays; I get interviewed by *The Atlantic*, by Eric Westervelt on National Public Radio, by our local newspaper. Parents email me and say, "I saw your interview in *The Atlantic*," and I think, "Oh, the one where I talked about batshit insane parents?" The pace of my work keeps increasing; I keep raising my hourly rate because at this point I don't even have room in my practice for new students and David points out that you raise your rates when demand outstrips supply, which it certainly seems to be doing.

And all along, I feel like a fraud. Parents hand me checks for hundreds of dollars (sometimes, they hand me envelopes of crisp $100 bills, which exacerbates the feeling that I'm doing something illicit). The money thing never stops being weird.

I work with first-generation students pro bono and slide the scale for families in need and stop sending invoices after a student's mother is diagnosed with an aggressive melanoma, but the unease persists. I work with families so wealthy that they have a personal assistant or a household manager who pays my bills, and those families I don't particularly worry about, but many of my students don't come from that kind of wealth. I feel deeply responsible when their kids don't get into their dream schools; one year, a brilliant, accomplished student I was pretty sure would get into at least a couple of Ivies, or MIT, or Duke, or a UC with a Regents Scholarship ends up "only" getting into the University of Virginia and UC San Diego, and I hate myself for thinking "only." I tell my students not to equate their self-worth with where they go to school, but I won't lie: I feel giddy when they get into thread-the-needle schools and guilty when they don't. I want colleges to see them the way I see them—funny, idiosyncratic, thoughtful, uniquely themselves—and when they don't, I feel like I haven't done my job. David tells me to think of myself as a batting coach: I can't make them hit the ball out of the park, I can't promise that they will hit the ball out of the park, but I can improve their hitting. This totally makes sense, except for the part where I can't help thinking that I'm not equal to the parents' expectations, that I can't be or do what they want, that I'm part of the problem, that I'm not worth what I charge, that I should be in a different line of work. When we go on hikes in the nearby foothills, Stanford's Hoover Tower looms above the valley like a reproachful exclamation mark.

I also figure out why some of the essays in the applications I read at Stanford were so uneven, and it's not, as I had assumed, because the student took less time writing and revising supplementary essays than the personal statement. Or maybe it is. But more likely, it's because the family either ran out of money or decided to stop working with whoever was helping the student with their essays. I've had parents who tell me that they didn't think the number of editing hours would be so high, even though I routinely tell families who work with me what to expect from the revision process and even though I routinely under-report the amount of time I spend on revisions or in meetings. The number of hours might be high for any number of reasons. It might be because the student decides to start a brand-new essay every time I send them comments instead of addressing those comments, and we have to start from scratch two or three times until I sit them down for a come-to-Jesus talk and tell them they have to stop being a serial starter and buckle down and deal with their shitty first draft, to borrow from Anne Lamott. Or it might be high because a student changes three words in a draft where I've written more than they did and decides to call it good, which might be not because they're lazy but because they're struggling with depression and debilitating anxiety.

I have a good innate sense for what I call a student's ceiling. If a student has worked through four or five drafts of an essay with extensive comments and discussion and advice and the essay still doesn't have a spark, I consider it done. Push past the ceiling, and the essay becomes mine, not the student's. I'm careful not to leave fingerprints, not to act as a ventriloquist, although I easily could. If we lock horns over what should or shouldn't be in the essay, I make sure to tell them the application is theirs, with their name on it, that their story is theirs to tell. And this is absolutely true, but it is also true that that story is, to some extent, bought, which means that people with more money get to tell the better story. It's not like I didn't already know this—history is written by the victors and all that—but it's one thing to know it and another thing entirely to experience it, to be part of a fundamentally unfair system and to despise it and benefit from it at the same time.

▶ Something you don't know about me is . . .

—UNIVERSITY OF MARYLAND

All happy families are alike, wrote Leo Tolstoy, and all unhappy families are unhappy in their own way.

By all appearances, we're a happy family. We post pictures on Facebook of the five of us at family camp, where David learns to walk on stilts, where Mara and Noah build forts from branches they find on the forest floor and try to catch the small fish that live in the lake, where Jordan and I play ping-pong, where we eat s'mores and sing "The Circle Game" at the evening campfire. I'm in my sixth year of running the book fair at the kids' elementary school. In high school, Jordan joins the wrestling team, and because he's 105 pounds at the start of high school and the team needs to fill every weight class, he immediately gets promoted to varsity. A local paper covers his first match and describes him as showing promise. Noah and Mara join the Eichler Gators, the same neighborhood summer swim team as Jordan, and all three of them spend hours at the pool swimming laps, practicing racing dives, and scarfing pizza at the weekly

Friday night pizza dinners. David signs up to be a volunteer coach and makes videos of each swim season, expertly scored to soundtracks that include "Tubthumping" and "Move It." We make sure all three kids are clean and neatly dressed and coach them to say please and thank you.

Our private lives are a different story. One July afternoon, when all three kids are home, I'm on the phone with a student while muted tussling, cursing, and other clear indicators of violence issue from the family room. Noah appears in my office doorway, looking at me with his big expressive brown eyes that speak volumes, but what he's trying to communicate I can't decipher because I am trying to explain to the student how she can transition from a paragraph where she describes teaching archery to autistic teens to a paragraph where she reflects on her own experience as a competitive archer. I briefly wonder why *my* autistic teen isn't doing something cool and productive like archery and then I remember, *Oh yeah, bows and arrows. No.*

I make crazy eyes at Noah and drag my hand across my throat to indicate that he, and whoever is in the other room, needs to shut the fuck up because I am on the phone with a student. Noah looks at me in disgust and leaves. More tussling sounds from the other room.

I hang up with the student just as my inbox lights up with an incoming message from Jordan. It reads: "While you were on the phone, Noah tried to steal the computer and when I tried to stop him he threatened me with a butter knife. Love, Jordan."

I forward the message to David with the subject line "Welcome to my own personal hell."

David responds: "Cool. Did Jordan try to defend himself with a melon baller?"

I fire back: "Ha ha. Laugh all you want. Noah stole your iPad."

David responds: "I'll have to attack him with a melon baller myself. Sick, sick child that one is."[22]

The same scenario happens the following morning, except that now I'm trying to edit essays online instead of discussing them by phone and instead of brandishing a butter knife (which he claims he did not actually brandish), Noah reportedly throws a Costco container of goldfish crackers at Jordan in what he later claims is an act of self-defense.

The remodel is finished and we have gleaming kitchen cabinets and drawers that don't rain sawdust and a shower with a mosaic inlay, and yet there are invisible cracks everywhere. Noah, who was never a motivated student, falls farther and farther behind in school and begins biting his fingernails to the quick and spends every free moment on the computer, a fleece blanket wrapped around him like a cocoon. We find a tutor who specializes in teaching study skills to students with executive functioning difficulties, and she meets with him every Wednesday, helping him stay organized, follow through, and plan ahead. He's his usual affable and compliant self and agrees to all the suggestions, but as soon as she leaves, out comes the blanket. We resort to confiscating the PlayStation, the computer, the phone, and he doesn't protest, just sits on the couch. I joke that with the dark gray blanket draped over his head, he looks like Emperor Palpatine and he glances at me blankly and says, "Ha ha."

Sometimes, I don't want to come home from work. At work, students hang on my every word. Parents tell me I have transformed their child, given her a sense of who she is, helped him discover his voice. At work, I can see the shimmering shape of the heart of an essay and know exactly

22. After many years of family therapy, David and I were utterly unsurprised to learn that humor is a coping mechanism, and that we tend to use our particular brand of dark humor to avoid talking about difficult feelings. Though I ask you: Who *wouldn't* choose cracking jokes over sitting with difficult feelings?

which questions to ask to bring that shimmering shape into being. At work, things make sense. They are under control. The students' actions have predictable outcomes. They study and they get good grades. They work through essay revisions and their essays become more insightful, more eloquent, more concise. Their efforts bear fruit—while at home, David and I wage a constant battle against entropy, which is a battle we seem destined to lose.

Our children are like the shoemaker's children in the proverb, except for the fact that we try our hardest to actually keep them in shoes. I took the admission job so I could spend more time with Jordan and Noah, and then with Mara; even now, my job allows me to be home most of the time. David and I don't travel for work, unlike many of the parents we know. Yes, we spend all day making shoes for other people, but those people are grateful for the shoes—pay us handsomely for the shoes, in fact—while our own children refuse to wear them, or drag them on the ground to slow their bikes down instead of using the brakes,[23] or otherwise destroy them.

One particularly bad evening David says to me, "I spend all day helping people, you know? And then I come home and I need to keep helping everyone, and whatever we do doesn't seem to work." Mara overhears him and says, "Poor daddy. He's like Charlie Bucket in *Charlie and the Chocolate Factory*," and I flash to the moment toward the end of *To the Lighthouse* when Lily Briscoe thinks about Mrs. Ramsay, "Mrs. Ramsay had given. Giving, giving, giving, she had died."

We go camping one weekend with a bunch of families from our swim club. Everything is going beautifully (redwood trees, long hikes, wine for the parents, s'mores for the kids), and then suddenly Jordan vanishes and no one

23. An actual thing that Mara started doing in middle school. If that's not a metaphor, I don't know what is.

knows where he is and the sun is going down and the forest all around us is turning dark and menacing and all the dads organize search parties and half an hour into the frenzy I come across Jordan at the far edge of the parking lot all the way across the camp site. He's completely oblivious to the commotion; he just wanted to go on a hike, he says. And David goes into our tent, ashen-faced, and says he has a headache and won't come out for the rest of the evening.

Apart from going to family camp every summer (that week in July is sacrosanct), we stop taking family vacations. Our home life is chaotic enough; after a disastrous trip to Los Angeles, we decide that taking the chaos on the road just isn't worth it.

Both David and I fret constantly that the mayhem at home is wrecking Noah and Mara's childhood. My hair starts to fall out, in large, alarming handfuls. I go to see the doctor, who asks, "Are you under any particular stress?" and I shrug and say, "You know, the usual." Occasionally, exhausted and spent at the end of another chaotic, dispiriting day, David and I go to bed and lay rigidly on our respective sides with the misery vibrating between us like an electric field. Even though the most intuitive thing would be to reach across the empty space in the middle, we're both afraid that if we did it would ignite, or implode, or explode, and consume us both, and so we don't.

▶ Respond to the following quotation in an essay of not more than 300 words: "Difficulty need not foreshadow despair or defeat. Rather, achievement can be all the more satisfying because of obstacles surmounted."

—AMHERST COLLEGE

I meet with a student who is in his second year at a local community college. He attended a local private high school—expensive, rigorous, known for placing students at prestigious colleges. Andy was not one of those students: he graduated with a 3.2 GPA and a lackluster resume and his parents—Taiwanese immigrants—refused to pay for an only so-so college, as his mother described UC Irvine. ("I had brought disgrace upon my family," he says with a sideways smile at our first meeting.)

At West Valley Community College, he got straight A's, became president of a social action club, and began volunteering for a nonprofit focused on mental health awareness among Asian American students. What prompted the turnaround, he told me with another crooked smile, was a job his parents made him take with Parks and Recreation the summer after he graduated from high school, as penance probably. As a junior employee, he was charged with unclogging an overflowing toilet in the men's room, and it was there, in that moment, that he flashed on the second line of *Moby-Dick,* which was pretty much as far as he'd gotten before skimming the rest of the novel for his senior English class: "Some years ago—never mind how long precisely—having little or no money in my purse, and nothing particular to interest me on shore, I thought I would sail about a little and see the watery part of the world." He tells me that as he plunged the toilet, it occurred to him that this was not the watery part of the world he wanted to see, and that epiphany prompted him to take school seriously. "It was like a virtuous cycle," he says. "The harder I worked, the more rewarding it became." I nod. I know about virtuous cycles.

I tell him he has to write an essay about this and he raises his eyebrows and says, "Really? About the clogged toilet, too?" I tell him absolutely about the clogged toilet, *and* about *Moby-Dick*. All of it. The first draft is over a thousand words long, and we work together to find the non-negotiable pieces and jettison the fluff, which I tell students is called "murdering your darlings." Cutting a draft is one of my favorite things to do; there's enormous satisfaction in figuring out how to compress sprawling ideas down to the word limit without losing their essence (my father, when I tell him about this, calls it "word engineering," trying to fit the same information into a smaller, more efficient envelope). After Andy finishes, he tells me that no one has ever paid so much attention to his writing before and confesses that he hated me until he understood what I was trying to do in my comments and that he's never been prouder of anything he's written. He gets into Berkeley with a Regents Scholarship, and I feel like, yeah, okay, maybe things *can* turn around.

▶ Tell us about something that is meaningful to you and why.

—STANFORD UNIVERSITY

Jordan enters senior year and suddenly everything seems to turn around, to click into place. I don't know if it's maturity or the salubrious effects of wrestling or something else, but David and I are stunned and grateful. He gets a driver's license and a job as a lifeguard at the city pool near our house; he is quickly promoted to head lifeguard, and he wakes up at 5:00 a.m. to drive himself to work and to wrestling meets (this after years of waking up late almost every school morning and rushing off to school amid yelling and mayhem). He studies for and takes the SAT and applies to college. His college essay is about being diagnosed with autism and about wrestling, and in it, he writes about being asked to make eye contact (the command, "Look at me," is a central part of the behavioral intervention curriculum) but notes that in wrestling, you're supposed to look at your opponent's feet for clues as to what he was going to do, not his eyes. He's admitted to University of the Pacific, and when he and David visit during admitted student day, he says, "I can see myself being a better person here."

These things happen so quickly that we almost don't have time to catch our breath, to register that he has beaten incredible odds, that none of this was supposed to happen. As a farewell gift, he gives us *The Naked Roommate: For Parents Only*, because, he tells us, it would have good tips for how to live without him in the house.

PART THREE
CONSEQUENCES

▶ What gets you excited about your academic interest selection(s)?

—POMONA COLLEGE

In his first semester at UOP, Jordan declares sports pedagogy as his major, makes the dean's list, and joins the club rugby team, where he is welcomed even though everyone else is about a foot taller and a hundred pounds heavier. We visit him during family weekend and take a family picture in front of the wrought-iron gate that says University of the Pacific and everyone is smiling and happy and it seems like this is it, finally, finally we're getting somewhere. For real this time.

Except that as Jordan's trajectory takes a sharp upward turn, Noah's continues to dip. He still swims for our local summer swim team, but he has tried and quickly quit high school swimming, lacrosse, and journalism. He continues to work with his study skills tutor and manages to squeak by with mostly B's in spite of doing very little, from what we can tell, but what worries us are not his grades but the fact that he has few interests—academic or otherwise—apart from video games and that he lacks initiative for pretty much anything except being comfortable. He does play complicated board games (Netrunner, Lords of Waterdeep, Star Wars X-Wing) with David and with his friends, and he is still good-natured and makes silly puns, and he occasionally writes elaborate, intricate Dungeons and Dragons adventures, but he doesn't finish them. Meanwhile, Mara comes home from middle school one day and mentions sheepishly that someone asked her where her older brother goes to college and that although she answered "UOP," they heard "UPenn" and she didn't correct them, because . . . you know.

I do know. Although David and I have made it clear that we don't care about prestige,[24] that what makes a college good is not its name or its reputation but whether it's good for the student who is attending, Mara has clearly been drinking the Palo Alto water. For her middle school peers, at least as she sees it, UOP doesn't sound nearly as good as UPenn, and to explain how mind-bogglingly amazing it is that Jordan is there in the first place means explaining the whole complicated backstory, and that is not something twelve-year-old Mara can or wants to do.

Not long after this conversation, we begin to notice changes in Mara too: although Jordan is away at college and doing well and the level of chaos at home has decreased dramatically, she is spending more and more time in her room with the door closed. She is reading less, unless you count Tumblr, in which case she's reading constantly. When David pulls out a board game or we turn on the TV and invite her to join us, she makes excuses and goes to another part of the house; at family get-togethers, she eats and leaves the table as

24. Okay, maybe we care about prestige a *little*. It's been thirty years, give or take, but on days when our sink is clogged or all three children are simultaneously in crisis or we have an ant invasion, I still occasionally tell David, "I gave up Princeton for this." Because reader, I did get into Princeton for graduate school, with a full scholarship and a stipend, and into Columbia, also with a full scholarship and a stipend, and David and I decided that the only realistic way to make marriage and grad school and medical school work was to go to UCLA, which was by far the cheapest option for both of us. But that doesn't mean that I'm entirely over it, and yes, I do sometimes wonder what would have happened if we had gone our separate ways, if I had gone to an Ivy League school. And then I think, "Nah."

soon as she can. When we try to engage her in conversation, she gets angry (which, together with withdrawn, is quickly becoming her default state), runs to her room, and slams the door, and we're left looking at each other across the dining room table at a total loss. A dull ache settles under my heart. No matter what I do—set out snacks after school, sit on the edge of her bed just to say hello, put an arm around her when she walks into the kitchen—I can't reach her.

I can't believe this is the same child who in third grade asked me to stand a little farther back from the classroom door during class dismissal so that she could get a running start and leap into my arms. ("Leap" was the word she used, and I melted into a puddle of goo right then and there.) I realize that she's twelve and no longer a child, but this change feels like something darker than the onset of adolescence, and we are yet again in uncharted waters and yet again nothing is going according to plan.

▶ What is something you thought you knew that you turned out to be wrong about? Why was this realization important?

—CLEMSON UNIVERSITY

Noah gets diagnosed with ADHD in his sophomore year; Mara gets diagnosed a year later, just as she's finishing middle school. In addition to ADHD, she is also given a diagnosis of depression and social anxiety, which, the psychiatrist tells us, often go hand-in-hand with ADHD. In ninth grade, she struggles in advanced geometry and has to drop down to regular geometry and, when that proves too challenging, even further down to algebra, which David and I don't care about but which makes her feel stupid and incompetent. She can't keep track of homework assignments, and she seems to think that leaving at the time you're supposed to be at your destination (which, in some cases, might be fifteen minutes away) means you're on time. We have screaming fights any time we have to be somewhere at a particular time—the orthodontist, a family birthday party, school.

It turns out that excellent Palo Alto schools are excellent primarily when it comes to high-achieving students on the AP track or students who need a great deal of structured support, so while students like Jordan, who had an individualized educational plan and the predictable and consistent demands of wrestling, make the most of high school, students like Mara and Noah fall through the cracks. They don't create disciplinary problems, nor are they in danger of dropping out, but they don't win awards or start nonprofits or get written up in the local paper, so they go largely ignored. The teachers who sense that they're struggling and who go out of their way to reach out to them are few and far between, and even those teachers can't seem to reach them.

I begin to wonder if David and I missed warning signs, if we should have done more. But what would that "more" be? More tutors, like everyone else in Palo Alto? More time stalking them on Schoology, the online portal where assignments and grades are posted? Helping them with homework any more than we have already tried to do in the face of their extravagant disinterest in completing an assignment, let alone completing it well? Forcing them into activities in which they evince not the slightest interest? Should we have sent Jordan away to boarding school and given Mara and Noah a shot at a normal childhood, whatever "normal" means? Should we have moved somewhere remote and rural, where they wouldn't have to compare themselves to Regeneron[25] Scholars or kids who read *Infinite Jest* or the collected works of Dickens for fun?

One day, out of the blue, I remember that Mr. Pelton, my senior-year English teacher, wrote "Surge on, young lady!" in my yearbook, and my heart contracts at the thought that we've launched Jordan but that Mara and Noah are not surging anywhere, and while my dreams don't have to be their dreams—I've read Khalil Gibran, I know that my children are not my children—it kills me that they don't seem to have dreams for themselves.

---

25. The Regeneron Science Talent Search is basically the Nobel Prize for teenagers.

I work with one of Noah's friends from elementary school, and the kid I remember as a friendly, charming goofball is now laser-focused on his future. He's still friendly and charming, but he is also sharp and articulate. He has spent his junior year in France, attending a French high school and becoming fluent, and now he wants to learn German and study international relations, with a particular focus on the European Union. He writes in his essay that he spent most of middle school playing video games and now he doesn't want to be that person anymore, and I can't help but think that Noah, who is also a rising senior, is still playing video games and seems unbothered in the slightest that his peers are moving on without him.

▶ Which book, character, song, or piece of work (fiction or non-fiction) represents you, and why?

—EMORY UNIVERSITY

To go to Whole Foods or Trader Joe's in North Palo Alto, I park off Alma between the two stores and walk to one or the other, sometimes both, because I can't abide the traffic in front of Whole Foods and I refuse to drive into the bedlam that is Town and Country shopping center where Trader Joe's is located. Whole Foods is for almond milk in the bulbous Calafia bottle and occasionally to visit the obliging butcher in the meat department who will cut a chicken into eight pieces and save me the entrails. Trader Joe's is for everything else, including the much cheaper vegetables and cheeses and wine and chocolate-covered almonds.

A few relics of yesteryear, like Peninsula Creamery and Heinichen's Automotive Repair, line the route, but mostly it's what I've taken to calling "start-up architecture" (post-Series B funding)—square or oblong new buildings faced with 12" × 12" squares of clashing-but-not slate tiles in ochre, gray, darker gray, slate, and countless shades of taupe. These tiles have names like California Gold, Three Rivers, China Multicolor, Lilac Kashmir, and Mongolian Spring, and they're designed to look like the rugged patchwork of a high desert landscape seen from a low-flying airplane: all those winding veins of gold and brown and gray and red and strips of iridescent yellow that could be wheat or actual gold or just ordinary pigmentation in elemental shades of copper, iron, bronze. The tiles get mixed reviews online—some reviewers say they're absolutely beautiful and others complain that about 5 percent are broken and 10 percent are completely worthless. Still others say that the percentage of tiles that are severely flawed and unusable is probably closer to twenty. My guess is that the same is true of the start-ups.

Sometimes, as I navigate the streets between Trader Joe's and Whole Foods, I pretend I'm wily Odysseus. My walk teems with twenty-first-century dangers: the stealthy Teslas and Priuses I can't hear coming; the woman in the Porsche making a right turn who can't be bothered to look through her oversized sunglasses to her actual right, where a pedestrian might be. In addition to the one that almost sideswipes me, I pass at least three more Porsches on the way: two Boxsters and one Cayenne. Lawn signs enact the strife over the local private girls' school that wants to expand its campus, located in a prime residential Palo Alto neighborhood. Some signs scream "Castilleja Put Your Plans On Hold" in angry blood-red letters; others, tacking sideways, claim diplomatically that the residents of this house "Support women's education." The striving for real estate and for excellence comes in layers—a nearby strip mall houses IVYMaxTutors (SAT II Prep! Editor! SAT/ACT! College Application Guidance!) in the first row of shops, closest to El Camino; a Mathnasium squats sullenly behind, in the second row. Also along El Camino, on the Stanford side, RVs line the curb like ships at anchor. That's where the unhoused people who are lucky live. The unluckier ones stand on medians at lights on busy streets, holding signs that say things like, "Hungry and too honest to steal. Please help." No one looks or listens, just like no one listened to Cassandra when she prophesied the destruction of Troy until it was too late. In the Stygian underpass on Embarcadero that takes me under the train tracks, I almost collide with a guy staring intently at his phone. He's wearing a Stanford Class of 2025 T-shirt, and because it's 2018 I have to pause to think: is he on a seven-year plan or is he simply just that confident? Another guy is screaming "All I really care about is the UI" into his Bluetooth headset so loudly that passers-by are turning to stare.

The moms at Trader Joe's, which is across the street from Palo Alto High School, look slightly dazed, like the Lotus Eaters. I look at them and think, *We've all eaten the lotus leaf; we were all duped; we all bought into the hollow dream of safety and success.* We moved to Palo Alto because the schools were good, and the schools devoured our children like Polyphemus devoured Odysseus' men, spitting out their bones. It's not just our family; it seems that no one's kids are happy. Almost every parent I speak to, at work or outside of work, says that they moved here for the schools only to find that the schools stretched their children to the breaking point, that all the joy has gone from their eyes. They say in a half-whisper that their heart skips a beat every time they hear the train whistle followed by a police siren.

At Trader Joe's, the bearded free-samples guy who retired from a career in tech but still wants to be around people is handing out miniature paper plates of quinoa salad in which dried cranberries glisten like rubies. The store is full of temptations, obstacles, adversaries; I duck into the cereal aisle to avoid the roving eye of a mom of a girl Mara was friends with in elementary school because I really, really don't feel like having a conversation about Mara's plans for next year or Emma's plans for next year or how competitive colleges are or who's doing what over the summer. I know how competitive colleges are. We will spend the summer tussling with Mara over whether or not it's appropriate to get out of bed at 2:00 p.m. on a weekday. I just want to get my goddamn organic arugula and turkey bacon and get the hell out of there.

In truth, I'm no Odysseus. I'm more of a Circe (not the alluring witch part; the part where I'm stuck in perpetual exile, gathering my herbs, weaving my stratagems, turning things into other things, helping scions of Bay Area royalty gain spots at highly coveted universities). Or maybe I have my metaphors wrong and it's not me who is Circe—it's this cursed town that lured us all in and then turned us into swine.

▶ Tell us about a significant challenge you've faced or something important that didn't go according to plan. How did you manage the situation?

—MIT

One sunny Saturday morning in April of his junior year, Jordan calls from UOP and tells me, apropos of nothing, that he's thinking of killing himself.

We know he's been struggling; his trajectory through UOP looks like a seismogram of a high-magnitude earthquake. After his fairy-tale first year, he rushed several fraternities but wasn't offered a bid, which devastated him; then he sustained two concussions in a row in rugby and had to quit the team, which devastated him further. By his junior year, he was no longer sure that he wanted to be a sports pedagogy major and accused David and me of forcing him into it; he complained that no one liked him and that he didn't know how to be around people; he became angry, irrational, resentful. We encouraged him to talk to someone at student psychological counseling services and to stay in touch with his mentor at the Office for Students with Disabilities, but the Office of Students with Disabilities was also a problem because Jordan didn't want to be a student with a disability. He wanted, as always, to be normal.

It's about 9:00 a.m.; David is still sleeping. I put the phone on speaker and google "what to say to someone who is suicidal" while Jordan tells me in a flat voice that he feels he has nothing to live for, that he has no friends, that he always wanted to do something big, like be president, but he recently realized none of these things would ever be possible. And shortly thereafter, I get an invitation via Google Docs to edit a document called "suicide note."

I click on the link with cold fingers and read the first line: "If you're reading this right now, I'm glad you got it." The rest is a blur—"there's no place for me in society . . . I'm very uncomfortable with myself and feel exposed every time I try to put myself out there." And then, at the end, "Maybe I'll see you in the afterlife lol."

Jordan does not commit suicide, but he talks about it ceaselessly over the next six months. We speak by Skype daily and he rages at us and tells us he is going to end it all, but then he relents and promises to check in again the next day. He refuses to take a medical leave from UOP and somehow passes all his classes, but he gains close to forty pounds because he's on an antipsychotic and shaves his head because he says he gets more attention that way. With his thick, bullish neck and the stubble on his head and his dead eyes, he looks disconcertingly like Jared Lee Loughner, the man who opened fire at a supermarket in Arizona, gravely wounding Gabby Giffords and killing a little girl. Jordan texts David and says he wants to drive 100 miles per hour and crash or get taken out by cops. He tells me he sometimes closes his eyes while driving on the freeway to see what would happen. He sends both of us ugly, combative texts blaming us for everything, and I can't help but think of Shakespeare's Caliban: "You taught me language, and my profit on't / Is I know how to curse."

In *The Tempest*, Prospero, the main character, is so absorbed in his books that he neglects the daily running of his kingdom, and his treacherous brother Antonio usurps his role, kidnaps him, and sets him and his baby daughter Miranda adrift on a raft. Prospero and Miranda wash up on an island; there, they find the spirit Ariel, imprisoned in a tree by the witch Sycorax, who has died, and the witch's son Caliban, neither man nor beast. Prospero uses his time on the island to perfect his magic and subdue both Ariel and Caliban, and when, by a stroke of fate, his former enemies sail close to the island, he creates a tempest that shipwrecks them on shore. There, in consummate control of the island and of the magic he has learned over twelve painstaking years, Prospero enacts a drama of revenge, redemption, and forgiveness.

Except that the only thing I seem to have in common with Prospero is burying my head in books while dark forces gather strength. I'm incapable of rough magic, of bending the elements to my will. And it seems that Jordan is out to enact his own drama of revenge and redemption—or to die trying—and the analogies don't hold, and none of the stories are unfolding the way they're supposed to.

When I taught *The Tempest* at UCLA, one of the themes we discussed, archly, because, ha ha, we were in a *literature* class, was that books are dangerous. They give you ridiculous ideas; they take you away from the real world and allow your enemies to take advantage of you. But perhaps our laughter was misguided; perhaps books, and book knowledge, really are dangerous things. Or at least they have been for me and David. Perhaps instead of reading books about behavioral intervention, we would have been better off leaving Jordan alone to his door-opening and door-closing self rather than teaching him to talk and forcing him into the neurotypical world to pretend that he was normal, until he couldn't pretend anymore.

He insists on returning to UOP in the fall, and after the brief respite of summer, things quickly deteriorate. Using his unerring radar for knowing what would upset those closest to him the most, Jordan announces that he's become a Trump supporter, acquires a red MAGA hat, and proclaims that everyone is "a dick," all women are "bitches," and Mexicans and Muslims need to get the hell out of America. He calls us in a towering rage because his whiteboard fell off the wall and he can't get it to stick back on, something that is clearly our fault because we never taught him anything. At last, we convince him to take a medical leave and come home so we can figure out, together, what to do next.

Somehow, David and I continue to go to work and maintain a cheerful demeanor at home and pretend, more or less successfully, that everything is fine, just fine, totally great. Until, in September, it's not fine. Jordan misses an appointment with his therapist and an appointment to complete the paperwork for a medical withdrawal from UOP and doesn't answer our calls or texts, and David calls campus police to ask to do a welfare check. For endless minutes, the two of us sit, staring at each other, until a cheerful campus police officer calls back and says that Jordan was just sleeping. At three thirty in the afternoon. In an apartment, which we find out the following day, when we come to pick him up, looks like a deranged person lives there.

Jordan is pale, puffy, unshaven (except for his head, which he has shaved again). He meets us at the door and without looking at either of us, mutters, "You made me like this," and stands aside to let us enter. The apartment is full of Jack in the Box wrappers, discarded pizza cartons, and overflowing garbage containers; at some point, he has just given up and started throwing garbage on the floor, which is covered with more takeout cartons and sour-smelling milkshake cups. The sliding closet door is off its hinges. There are dirty clothes everywhere. David and Jordan drive home in Jordan's car, and I follow in ours, crying the entire ninety-three minutes of the drive, which I believe is a record for me.

We see another educational consultant in early October, and I text David from her waiting room to let him know that she recommended sending Jordan to a wilderness therapy program.

David responds, "Wilderness, wilderness. Like a Shakespeare character he can enter the wilderness to work out the problems of city and home."

"Caliban was in the wilderness and a fat lot of good it did him," I write back.

"So was Lear and he got naked," David writes. "So maybe not Shakespeare. How about Emerson? Nature, pond, introspection, etc."

I tell David he's thinking of Thoreau and invoke my favorite summary of *Walden*: man sits by pond for two years. Nothing happens except he writes the most boring book in the world with only a couple of good lines.

David answers that we should "Thoreau" Jordan into the wilderness, which makes me laugh for the first time in what feels like years, and three days later, as though some malign intelligence is affronted by that moment of levity, Jordan tries to commit suicide.

What happens is this: Jordan—who is visiting my parents in San Francisco so that we can take a break from each other—tells them he's going for a walk. An hour later, my mom, worried by his long absence, calls and asks me to look him up on Google Locate. Google Locate shows him on Broderick and Chestnut, completely the wrong direction from my parents, as of nine minutes before I track him. And when the phone refreshes it shows him at the foot of the Golden Gate Bridge. Which he had, on more than one occasion, talked about jumping off. The day before he left for my parents' on October 12, he had added up the minutes and seconds and hours and days of his life and mentioned offhandedly how funny it would be if the day of his birth was also the day of his death. His birthday is October 14.

I stand in the kitchen feeling oddly, preternaturally calm—so much so that I can feel my fingers tingling and my heart beating, slowly and violently—as I stare at the blue dot that represents Jordan in exactly the wrong place, at exactly the wrong time. I hang up with my mom and dial 911, which patches me through to the CHP, which intercepts Jordan a half hour later and puts him on a 5150 hold at Cal Pacific Medical Center.

On his actual birthday, Jordan gets transferred to Good Samaritan in Los Gatos, which as far as locked wards go is a mellow place with really nice nurses, according to David, anyway. One of those nurses tells Jordan when he was first checked in that he needed to go swim in the ocean (apparently, she was unaware that he had thought about trying to do just that, albeit from a great height). She tells us the same thing, adding that nature is the best medicine, away from computers and phones, and we don't disagree. By then, the educational consultant has found a wilderness program in Utah that will accept him as soon as his seventy-two-hour hold is over.

Jordan turns twenty-two at Good Sam, wearing flip-flops and pants with no belt. We come bearing half a Trader Joe's chocolate bar (because we don't have the time, or the wherewithal, to get anything else), and I tell him that maybe this would be the birth of a new Jordan. "Maybe," he replies skeptically.

It's overcast when we drive home from Good Sam. There are black birds clustered on the telephone wires over the freeway, like a phrase in an arcane language or a spell I can't for the life of me decipher.

▶ (Optional) If you think that additional information about your family will give us a more thorough impression of your background, please include it here.

—MIT

Both my grandmothers lost a little boy before my parents were born. Grandma Ester's son, Valeriy, was born in 1941, a few months after they fled their hometown just hours ahead of the advancing Germans. He died of pneumonia in 1943, in a remote village near Kazakhstan where my grandparents lived crammed into provisional housing with other refugees. There was no heat and no running water and scarcely anything to eat except an occasional potato, and certainly no medicine. Grandma Tsilya's son, my father's older brother, died before the war, also at two, but beyond that, no one in our family knows anything—not his name, not why he died. She never spoke of him when she was alive, and now that she's gone, there is no one to ask.

For both my grandmothers, worrying about *deti*, the children, was a full-time occupation. Although David scoffs at the idea of inherited trauma, I believe in it with every fiber of my being. The Russian word for worry is *volneniye*, from the word *volna*, wave; it literally means agitation, disturbance, the state of being unstill. The verb, *volnovatsya*, was passed on to me along with my mother's milk and formed the contrapuntal refrain of my otherwise carefree childhood. The need to keep children safe is in my bones; I can hear the whispering ghosts of the two little boys my grandmothers lost and of my drowned cousin and of the boy on whose bones Stanford is built.

But what does it mean, really, to keep a child safe? Does it mean smoothing the road ahead of them, padding the corners, protecting them from disappointment, or does it mean putting them in a leaky boat on an ocean or pushing them into the thickets to find their own way or subjecting them to trials of strength and wit? After Jordan's diagnosis, did we overstep in declaring our own personal war on autism, in redirecting his behaviors, in pushing him to talk, to reach out to other children, to do things that were fundamentally out of character for him—all, ostensibly, in the service of giving him more options and helping him lead a better, more meaningful life? And once he tells us he doesn't want to be alive, doesn't see a place for himself in the world, how can we not think that this is somehow our fault, that we have taught him enough for him to understand that he is somehow lacking but not enough to do something about it? Are we all that different from the relentlessly ambitious parents of my students, or the dozens of other parents snared in Operation Varsity Blues—and the hundreds if not thousands of other parents who haven't been caught?

Charles Blow once wrote that the grandmother who raised him understood that good parenting is like giving a hug: love and pressure and there's no right way to do it. But what to do when the love becomes suffocating, when the pressure cripples, when good intentions curdle into malignancy? What to do when you realize that in thinking you were helping your child, you were all the while pushing them closer to the edge of the abyss?

It seems centuries have passed since I thrilled to the feel of the word *chthonic* in my mouth. At the time, I believed myself to be invulnerable to the calamities that befell others, to the malevolence of the fates and the furies. Catastrophe by water, by bullet, by disease, by hunger, by being in the wrong place at the wrong time—that was neither for me nor for my children. Never did I dream that the undoing would come, like it always does, from within, from what I cherished most about myself: my erudition, my vigilance, my good intentions.

▶ What is your greatest talent or skill?

—UNIVERSITY OF CALIFORNIA PERSONAL INSIGHT QUESTION

Jamie, one of my students, is writing an essay about growing up across the street from a park with an old-fashioned playground—the kind with a metal slide that would burn you in the summer and a rusted merry-go-round and a see-saw guaranteed to give you splinters or tetanus or both, the kind where she once found what she describes as "a half-filled water balloon" in the sandbox, which her mother snatched out of her hands, yelling "No, no, no, no!" while dragging her home, where she made her wash her hands for ten minutes. I find this anecdote hilarious, especially because it serves as a poignant counterpoint to what follows—a thoughtful reflection on her loss of confidence in high school and her longing for her intrepid childhood—but her school counselor says that Yale, where Jamie is applying, is not going to be amused by a story about finding a used condom in a sandbox.

This is what I'm good at: helping students find the memorable detail; helping them hold their ground against adults who try to smooth the grain of their writing; helping them push the envelope, but never too far. Jamie is brilliant; her accomplishments are clear in her grades, in her glowing letters of recommendation (all of her teachers volunteered to write for her before she even asked them), in her résumé, in the fact that she is reading Schopenhauer and Kant in her free time. Given these credentials, she can afford to reference a used condom without actually naming it, and more than anything I love how slyly she manages to capture it through her six-year-old eyes, because of course a six-year-old would see a half-filled water balloon and not a condom. I tell her all this, and then tell her to decide based on what feels true to her, not on what others want her to do.[26]

Next to Jamie's essay is a tab with an essay by another student, one whose older sister told her not to write about her struggle with an eating disorder because doing so would result in an automatic no and Marissa wants more than anything to go to Dartmouth so she is not sure what to do. She's a prodigiously gifted writer whose essay about her volunteer work at an eating disorders clinic in her hometown falls utterly flat because conspicuously missing from it is why she volunteers there in the first place. Marissa will tell me that she considers herself fully recovered; that her eating disorder occurred in seventh and eighth grade; that part of her recovery was understanding that for her Hungarian-born parents, mental health challenges presented a devastating stigma; that initially, when she began her volunteer work, her parents were deeply opposed; and that one day, she looked up at the end of a presentation about eating disorders at her church and saw, behind the four other people in the audience, her mother in the back wiping away tears. I tell her to put all that in the essay and decide which version seems truest, and she sends the one with the full story.[27]

Next to that is a tab with my gmail, where I have emails waiting: one from a mother of a student who has just been

---

26 She sends the unredacted essay, and apparently Yale does not mind at all.

27 And gets admitted.

diagnosed with depression and learning differences in the middle of his junior year, five with essay drafts (one of the essays sounds nothing like the student, and I will find out later that his parents hired an older cousin to "help" even though he is already working with me)[28], an email from the therapeutic wilderness program in Utah where Jordan is now enrolled, an email about parent weekend from CSU Chico (where Noah is now a freshman and which he is going to leave after freshman year), and an email from Palo Alto High School warning me that Mara now has thirty-two tardies in the space of two months and that the school will refer us to the district attorney's office because she is now considered a truant.

And this is where I fail: in knowing how to reach my children. With my students, I have a rapport so strong it feels nearly telepathic, but my own children are opaque, impenetrable. I don't know how to talk to them. When I try, I feel tongue-tied and clumsy. They perceive advice as criticism, questions as nagging, hugs as intrusions. Mara in particular may as well be covered in thorns.

It used to be easier. Apparently the saying "Little kids, little problems; big kids, big problems" is true. When he was in sixth grade, Jordan read *The Hobbit* and came to me full of questions about why Bilbo spares Gollum's life when he could have just as easily stabbed him from behind; we talked for a long time about empathy, about Bilbo pausing to imagine what it must have been like to be Gollum, to live in darkness and fear day after day. That same year, Jordan spent

28. The essay is almost laughably bad—hyperbolic, insincere, with a moral so glaringly obvious it might as well be outlined in neon. When the student and I meet and he explains its provenance, I ask him if he understands how dishonest it would be to submit someone else's writing. He says he does but adds that his parents have told him not to be stupid, that everyone cheats. (He ends up submitting his own essay, where he draws deft connections between Vanity Fair and his status-obsessed family, and is admitted to Vanderbilt, Princeton, and Tufts.)

an hour in the pool patiently walking me through the steps of a flip turn until I mastered it. (David, who swam in high school and played water polo in college, had given up after multiple attempts, saying I was unteachable; so had Sue, the swim team coach). Noah and Mara and I laughed together when I read *The True Meaning of Smek Day* out loud to them using funny voices for the aliens. When she was seven or eight, Mara made Jordan a plate of chocolate pieces after he lost a tough wrestling match. On the plate was a note: "To Jordan, who tried so hard and deserved to win."

With my students, we have a common goal: they want to apply to college, and I want to help them create the most compelling possible application. With my children, it feels like we're working at cross-purposes; we want to help them, whereas they don't want to be helped. Or, and this is immeasurably worse, they don't want to be helped by *us*.

PART FOUR
ADMISSIONS

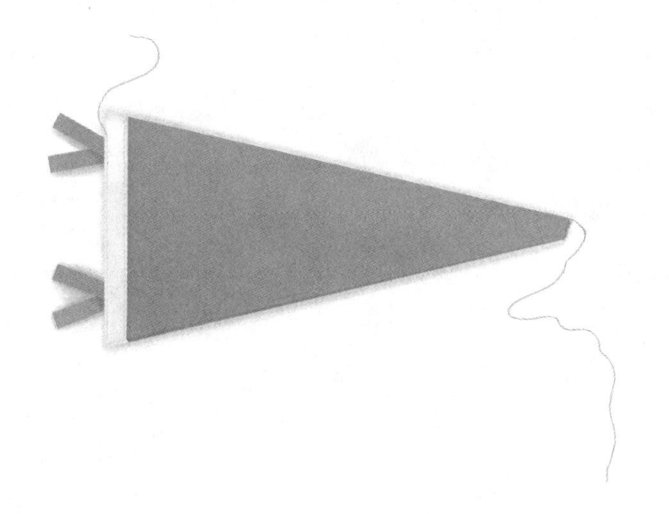

▶ Describe a problem you've solved or a problem you'd like to solve. It can be an intellectual challenge, a research question, or something you encountered in school—anything that is of importance to you, no matter the scale. Explain its significance to you and what steps you took or could take to identify a solution.

—COMMON APP PERSONAL STATEMENT PROMPT

Our children are not the problem, and we're not the problem. The problem is the problem, as therapists like to say. The problem is that I am a college admissions consultant and David is a psychiatrist and our children don't move effortlessly through the world and we live in a place where it seems everyone else's children do. The problem is that we care about what people think, both of us and of our children. The problem is that while I am a ringer at extricating the pearl from the oyster when it comes to college essays, I have no words for what I'm living through. There's no pearl, only a slippery, amorphous mass.

When Jordan was first diagnosed, we received a referral to a parent support group, but we went to only one meeting before deciding it was not for us. The other parents looked defeated and hopeless and had older children with bigger problems we did not want to begin to contemplate. David and

I were raring to embark on a heroic journey to save our child and the other parents looked like they wanted to sit dejectedly on a park bench and feed the pigeons. Now, as Noah and Mara struggle, we don't even know what kind of support group we could find—one for parents of multiple children with neurological differences? For parents of children who refuse to get out of bed or who wrap themselves in a blanket and spend all day in front of the computer or who clearly have the innate capacity to do well in school but don't? And even if we were to find a support group, we wouldn't be able to go anyway, because we're too busy putting out fires at home[29] and working to pay for our insurance (which is monstrously expensive because we're both self-employed) and for therapists and psychiatrists for our children, which our monstrously expensive insurance covers only fractionally.

Therapy is also out. Confiding problems to other people is not something I do easily. I saw a therapist for a couple of months during an episode of postpartum depression after Jordan was born, and that and a Zoloft prescription helped. But given how little discretionary time I have, an ongoing relationship with a therapist doesn't seem viable. Instead, I compulsively play Words with Friends on my phone (because arranging letters into high-scoring words without having to do the math like you have to in Scrabble is almost as satisfying as arranging words in student essays). I go on long walks around the neighborhood, mulling over what might be to blame for the slowly unfolding catastrophe of our home life. Could it be the malathion that helicopters sprayed all over the Bay Area to battle an epic fruit fly infestation when I was thirteen? The

29. Metaphorical as well as actual fires. When Jordan was in middle school, he put an electric kettle on the stove to heat up some water while David was taking a nap, causing a pretty spectacular plastic/electrical conflagration. And Mara, also in middle school, swept some still-smoldering incense into her wastebasket and, when the fire alarm went off, shoved it in her closet because she was convinced that I would get mad at her. Fortunately, I managed to discover the conflagration before our house burned down.

Northridge earthquake that happened right around the time Jordan was conceived? The fact that I was teaching at Stanford *and* shadowing Jordan at preschool *and* trying to make sure he was learning as much as possible in his at-home behavioral program while I was pregnant with Noah? The fact that I worried about Jordan *and* Noah *and* David, who was still grieving for his dad, while I was pregnant with Mara? The fact that it always seems like we're not doing enough, that in trying to help one of our children we somehow harm another, that there isn't enough of us to go around?

I come from a long line of people who are experts at bottling things up. My paternal grandfather drowned when my father was thirteen, and my widowed grandmother told no one other than immediate family that she had lost her husband because she was convinced people would think that she or my thirteen-year-old father or his eight-year-old brother had done something to deserve it. I avoid speaking to my parents about what is happening at home—it will just upset them, and what can they do about it anyway? When I do talk to them, I find that I lack the vocabulary to describe what is happening. In Russian, the catch-all term for any kind of noticeable neurological difference is *defektivniy*, defective, and this is a word none of us want to use. After Jordan was diagnosed, my parents urged me not to tell other people that he had autism; we never did tell either of his great-grandmothers. We tell very few people that Jordan was suicidally depressed and is now in a therapeutic wilderness program; hardly anyone knows that we spend hours each week writing letters to him and poring over the letters he writes to us, that both Mara and Noah see therapists, that in spite of therapy and medications and tutors and hiding electronics and forcing them to go on family hikes they seem to be stalled in place, if not regressing.

The problem is that David and I are advice-giving people and our children have no use for our advice, and the more urgently compelled we are to press our advice upon them the more they resist. The problem is that David, who specializes in psychopharmacology for mood disorders, knows worst-case outcomes for what our children are going through but is powerless to do anything about it because doctors aren't supposed to treat their own children. The problem is that we don't recognize ourselves in any of our kids and isn't that what having children is for—to make newer, better versions of ourselves? The problem is that Mara has stopped reading books altogether, except for Tumblr and now an old *Diagnostic and Statistical Manual of Mental Disorders* that David has lying around, but she refuses to tell us what she's reading about and why. The problem is that all of us are stuck, just in different ways.

It's not always terrible. When Mara finally gets out of bed and wanders around in a long T-shirt and I ask her to put on pants, she says, "Pants? In this economy?" She makes videos about the comings and goings of our cats, with wry, choppy background commentary in which I recognize my own snark, but the sharpness and deadpan humor are all hers. We take Mara and Noah on vacation to New Orleans, where we go on a swamp tour and wander around the French Quarter and listen to jazz in Preservation Hall and where David, Mara, and Noah make fun of me for dragging them on a boring tour of historic houses in the Garden District and David, Mara, and I make fun of Noah who is outraged because a waitress brings a ramekin of ketchup as soon as he orders but takes a long time to bring the actual burger and fries, which he takes as a personal affront and threatens to write a bad Yelp review.[30] We watch *Freaks and Geeks* and *The Goldbergs* and *Raising Arizona* together. Occasionally, during bright,

30. The review is still pending. In it, Noah is planning to hold forth on the appropriate delivery of ketchup to delivery of burger ratio, which he claims should be ten minutes at the most. The waitress took at least seventeen, which in Noah's opinion is just taunting the customer.

teasing moments we'll sit down and play a board game. David is amassing a veritable library of board games—Settlers of Catan, Lords of Waterdeep, Finca, Istanbul, Splendor, Ticket to Ride. The board games are beautiful, each one a window into an orderly universe with predictable rules and pieces that move in accordance to those rules, and when David plays them his face relaxes.

And then one Father's Day, after we've had dinner and we're about to play a new board game that was his Father's Day present, Mara spills hot tea all over the jewel-bright game cards and intricately illustrated board, after repeated warnings not to perch her teacup on the side of her plate where it was perched precariously in spite of the warnings, and David lets out a strangled—I don't know what. (I'm tapping again at that amorphous mass.) Not a cry, exactly, and not a bellow, and not a shout, but a sound so primal, so full of rage and grief and anguish that Noah and Mara scatter and he and I are left to mop up the damage as best we can and there's no world in which I can think, *It's only a game.*

▶ If you could change one thing to better your community, what would it be? Why is it important and how would you contribute to this change?

—UNIVERSITY OF NORTH CAROLINA CHAPEL HILL

"Happy holidays, everyone!

"What a year 2016 has been for our family! David and I have been hard at work as always; Mara is in her freshman year at Palo Alto High School and might set a record for most tardies received in a month; Noah started his freshman year at CSU Chico, where we suspect he is floundering though he reassures us he's not, so fingers crossed! Our big excitement this year was that Jordan fell into a deep depression in the spring (T. S. Eliot was spot on: April *is* the cruelest month!) and came close to committing suicide (even though he claims he had just gone to the Golden Gate Bridge to do some sightseeing, LOL). But luckily, he didn't (scary, though, right?), and we found a wilderness program in Utah that literally saved his life.

"Not that any of your children are likely to need the services of a therapeutic wilderness program (judging by your holiday cards, you're all doing great, so mazel tov!), but if you do, Aspiro is top-notch. You don't even need to send your kid with any equipment—just the clothes on his back and his medications. They provide everything—sleeping bags, hiking boots, jackets, pants, sweatshirts, underwear—as well as a therapist who will meet with your kid weekly and be kind and firm and grounded and call him on his bullshit when needed. Your kid lives outside 24/7—yes, even in the winter!—learning to keep himself warm, prepare his own food, and get along with other equally troubled young adults. (I mean, aren't we all struggling with something?)"

This is the holiday newsletter I start composing in my head in early December 2016[31] as our mailbox fills with holiday cards from friends, neighbors, former classmates. But then, after the second paragraph, I hit a wall. Sarcasm, snark, dark humor—favorite tools in my arsenal—can't help me here. What we're living through is too dark. Too big, too hard to explain, too complicated, too tender.

2016 was a year of catastrophe. Grandma Ester died in January. In April, Jordan told us he wanted to kill himself. In the same month, one of my former students did kill herself. A close friend's husband cheated on her and killed a pedestrian while driving drunk after she kicked him out. An Oakland warehouse that had been converted into an artist collective caught fire and thirty-six people perished. But this December, just like every other December, our mailbox overflows with holiday cards. The ones that are photos only I don't mind, but the ones with newsy updates—we're thriving, our children are thriving, here's us on vacation, here's us helping our kid move into her first apartment—are like salt on a wound.

We've never sent out a holiday card. Not because we don't take a good picture (we do, as it happens), but because it feels wrong to tell the world we're fine when we're emphatically not. But in December, David and I fly to Utah for a

31. Inspired by David Sedaris's holiday masterpiece, "Season's Greetings to Our Friends and Family!!!"

parent seminar, where we're going to see Jordan for the first time in months and meet about twenty other parents who have also come to Utah to see their children. That's how I introduce myself: by saying that our house is full of holiday cards and that just once, I wish I could write the absolutely 100 percent true Smith holiday newsletter, something that starts with "Hey everyone, what a year it's been for our family!" Everyone cracks up, and just like that, I feel like, hey, these are my people.

It's been two months since we put Jordan, forlorn and stubble-headed, wearing too-tight jeans and a red sweatshirt, on a plane to Salt Lake City. Apart from learning to survive in the wilderness, he has spent that time learning self-efficacy and positive coping strategies. And then he walks through the door of the conference room, red-cheeked, bearded, forty pounds lighter, in black snow pants and a black parka, and when he sees us, his face lights up, and he rushes toward us, and something in me unclenches. We come together in a real hug, not one where Jordan stiffens, not where he leads with the shoulder, but a hug that lasts a long, long time. And at the lunch buffet, even though he's eaten nothing but trail food since he got to Utah, he motions me and David to go ahead of him.

Aspiro has a tradition called "gratitude letters," where both the parents and the children are asked to write a letter detailing their journey and the things that they're grateful for and read those letters to each other on the last day of the seminar. Weirdly, we all reference J. R. R. Tolkien. I talk about how Jordan was an adventurous eater, muttering "raw fish for supper" after his discovery of sushi; David quotes Bilbo ("I'm going on an adventure!"); Jordan mentions reading *The Hobbit* and watching *The Lord of the Rings* trilogy with David, who is a die-hard Tolkien fan.

Jordan's nine-page letter, written in his laborious scrawl, is unexpectedly funny (he mentions his "very handsome beard" and thanks David for using his earnings to help support him instead of building a big mansion and me for "taking one for the team" by going into college consulting and making delicious food). He writes that he was becoming an upstanding young adult, and thanks us for not giving up on him. And he signs it, "Your son, Jordan Smith," in case, you know, we didn't remember.

It's cold and bright in the room where we read the gratitude letters, and David shivers in his thin blue shirt as Jordan reads. Or maybe I'm the one who is shivering, and maybe it isn't even because of the cold. I'm thinking of Sam's words to Frodo about the great stories, the ones full of darkness and danger, the ones where you didn't want to know the end, because it seemed impossible that the end could be happy. But in the end, Sam says, the folks in those stories kept going because there's some good in this world and it's worth fighting for.

It's easy to believe that there's some good in this world as we sit together, shoulders touching. Snow is falling outside. There's a palpable stillness and softness in the room, and the three of us are afraid to move too quickly or talk too loud for fear of disturbing it. It's been so long since I've felt hope, but there it is, this unfamiliar fluttering in my chest.[32]

---

32. We still don't send holiday cards, but now, I look at the holiday cards that come in the mail every December and wonder: What pain might be hiding behind the smiles? What *isn't* reported in the year-in-review updates? Perhaps others are struggling too, but they're tough enough and organized enough to put on happy faces and make picture collages on Shutterfly or TinyPrints and print out address labels and get all the cards in the mail by mid-December. This is not a feat I'm equal to, although I do still occasionally fantasize about sending a truthful holiday card, just like I fantasize about doing stand up and shouting all my ugly truths—with the obligatory snarky twist—from the stage, or being on *Fresh Air* with Terry Gross (Hi, Terry, if you're reading this, I love your show and I'm available anytime!), or about being four inches taller. Or, here's an idea: we could declare a moratorium on holiday cards altogether. Think how much heartache and aggravation such a moratorium could save, not to mention paper and postage.

▶ Has there been a time when you've had a long-cherished or accepted belief challenged? How did you respond? How did the challenge affect your beliefs?

—COALITION ESSAY PROMPT

Many of my students' parents are immigrants. They sometimes come from deep poverty; they are often engineers or doctors; they have worked tirelessly to become who they are, and now they want their children to go to schools whose names they sometimes misspell (Standford, Berkley, Colombia) but pronounce with breathless reverence because those names are synonymous with success, with validation, with proof that they have made the right choices and done the right things. Their need is palpable and stifling; they are willing to do anything, including paying thousands of dollars to me, to test-prep tutors, to expensive summer programs. They are willing to overlook that this single-mindedness may be hurting their child, because while some students thrive under this kind of pressure, others develop eating disorders, anxiety, depression, OCD. They stop sleeping and smiling. Sleeping and smiling are for later. They are willing to defer gratification in exchange for a success story, and where I live, a success story ends with the acronym HYPS.

College admission in highly selective colleges and universities gives the lie to everything students and their parents have been led to believe: the aspirational narratives of the American dream, the pull-yourself-up-by-the-bootstraps Horatio Alger story. You can do all the right things—prenatal vitamins, Baby Einstein, enrichment classes, "gifted and talented" programs, piano, violin, soccer, swimming, baseball, basketball, private school, voice lessons, math camp, band camp, debate camp, private school, SAT prep—and not get what you were expecting, indeed, what you may have believed you were entitled to. College admission is arbitrary and howlingly unfair. As a matter of fact, it's a lot like life.

Before I became a parent, I saw the world much like my students' parents do: as a logical, predictable place where certain actions yield predictable consequences. Having children upended that notion; it's entirely possible, it turns out, for two intelligent, high-functioning, ambitious people to have not one, not two, but three children whose neurological wiring makes it extraordinarily difficult for them to function in the world, and whose trajectory, as a result, will be anything but linear. It took a while—okay, a couple of decades—to come to terms with the disjunction between what we expected and what we got. When Jordan was first diagnosed with autism, David and I refused to read Emily Kingsley's "Welcome to Holland"[33] and instead read parent memoirs about "beating" autism, about children who had

33. A 1987 essay about having a child with Down Syndrome. In it, Kingsley writes that expecting a baby feels like being aquiver with anticipation on a flight to Paris (the Eiffel Tower! The Louvre! Baguettes by the Seine!)—only when the plane lands, the pilot says, "Welcome to Holland" (aka, the Land of Special Needs). Holland, Kingsley writes, is also beautiful, just in a different way, and you will learn to love the windmills and the tulips, once your grief and disappointment subside. And David and I were like, "Fuck no, we wanted baguettes by the Seine."

gone from nonverbal and detached to indistinguishable from any other child, and we imagined ourselves as those parents, only better. In those first few shell-shocked days, a well-meaning friend tried to talk us down from our adrenaline-spiked anguish, a borderline manic state in which it seemed imperative to do as much as possible as quickly as possible because the toddler brain was plastic and malleable, meaning that we could teach Jordan all kinds of things really quickly, transforming his brain through repetition or cutting new neural pathways or something. He told us, speaking carefully, like one does to crazy people, that in a few months this would all settle in and we would be extraordinarily savvy parents of an autistic child.

But we brushed his words off; we wanted to be extraordinarily savvy parents, yes, but not of an autistic child. And yet that was the child we got. In learning to live with him—and with his siblings—I have tried to cultivate both a sympathy for and a detachment from the parents who live to have their child turn out a certain way and whose aspirations I recognize on a cellular level. They sit in my office and ask me, with desperate hope in their eyes, "Is there anything else we can do?" ("We" is not a good sign.)

No one wants to hear that you can do all the right things and not get into Harvard, Stanford, Princeton, Caltech, MIT. No one wants to live in a world where causality is not a thing, where rules don't apply. No one wants to believe that doing all the right things guarantees nothing. They tell me about their neighbor's son or their cousin's daughter, the one who spent the summer at Johns Hopkins or who started a nonprofit or who took this one class and is now at Harvard, and the unspoken hope is that I will figure out some kind of magic potion or formula to get the kid into Harvard too.

When I started working as an independent counselor, the neediness used to set my teeth on edge. I fantasized about screaming, "Do you know what I'm dealing with at home? Do you really think your daughter's A- in AP US History is a crisis? Did you really need to title your email "URGENT IMMEDIATE REPLY REQUESTED" because your son wasn't admitted to a summer program that accepts about 2.5 percent of all applicants?" Now I nod in recognition—not because I don't think they're being absurd (I do), but because I get it. Their desperation was David's and my desperation when we pushed Jordan to "touch blue," when we set up carefully scripted playdates, when we held tortilla chips out of reach at Chevy's so he would ask for them, when we badgered Noah about living up to his potential, when we drew up behavioral contracts with Mara.[34] At our core, we're exactly the same. Every parent wants their children to land well in the world. We want them to be seen and to be recognized and to be, yes, accepted, whether that means making it to Yale or making eye contact, getting into Princeton or getting out of bed.

On particularly difficult days, I find comfort in centuries of stories about wayward, headstrong children and grasping, driven parents. Greek myths, Clytemnestra and Orestes, Creon and Haemon, Lear and his daughters. The entire Old Testament. Fairy tales. I remind myself of James Baldwin's words—"You think your pain and your heartbreak are unprecedented in the history of the world, but then you read." There's comfort in that, in knowing that invisible threads connect us all, that we are more alike than we think.

34. Behavioral contracts are bullshit and don't work.

▶ USC faculty place an emphasis on interdisciplinary academic opportunities. Describe something outside of your intended academic focus about which you are interested in learning.

—USC

Jordan moves back home in early 2017 after finishing the wilderness program. He's decided to get his bearings before finishing UOP, and although the first few months of living with him are tenuous, gradually, we get into a rhythm. Jordan drives Mara to school and to her job at a fancy chocolate shop in downtown Palo Alto; on his own, he finds a nearby jujitsu studio where he works out several times a week; he signs up for psychology, rhetorical writing, and ballroom dancing[35] at the local community college. Over dinner, he explains to us that he's learning how to use pathos, logos, and ethos in persuasive writing and asks David questions about personality disorders. At the end of the quarter, he invites us to a dance department showcase where his class performs a complex choreographed group number in which all the women wear black tops and silver skirts and all the men wear black shirts, black pants, and

35. No, this is not like *Silver Linings Playbook*.

spangled silver vests. He and his partner move through the dance sequence without a single glitch, as far as I can tell. Jordan isn't graceful exactly, but he's earnest and determined and it's clear that he and his partner have practiced for hours, and there's something about the sight of him on stage in that spangled silver vest that just totally undoes me.

It's around this time that I start trying to write about our family. I've been writing desultorily for years, starting when Jordan was about five years old. He had made such remarkable progress so quickly that I decided I would write a "how we beat autism" book, and that it would be nothing like the saccharine memoirs we've read about other "recovered" autistic children. No, it would be snarky and smart and full of black humor, like David Sedaris if David Sedaris were a short Russian-Jewish woman with an autistic child. But that was before I started working in admissions, before we had Noah and Mara, before everything started going off the rails. I show the stories I've been writing to Elyse, my co-editor, who also happens to be a prodigiously gifted poet and writer and editor, and she tells me that many of the stories I've written have pat endings (what she actually says is that at times the endings choose humor or a "lessons learned" pronouncement rather than the messier, darker explorations of my experience), but I don't want them to be complicated. And so I leave out, at least in the early drafts, the part where Noah fails out of CSU Chico after one year because, after a promising start (he even emails me in early fall to get my thoughts about his paper on Ovid's *Metamorphoses* for his honors seminar), he mostly stays in his room playing video games and fails all his classes. I don't write about how he gets fired from his first job as a result of constantly being on his phone, and then his second job, also as a result of being on his phone, and then, because David and I no longer know what to do, we tell him that he can either enlist in the military or go to Aspiro, the same wilderness program Jordan had gone to, and he chooses Aspiro. I leave out our gnawing disquiet about Mara. I want a teleological narrative, where struggles have purpose and meaning ("We must suffer, suffer into truth," Aeschylus wrote), because if the struggles are only that—struggles with no redemption—then what good is anything? The world would be meaningless, like the episode of *The Simpsons* where the family casts about for a moral to explain a series of increasingly absurd events until Lisa suggests that perhaps there is no moral. "Exactly," Homer chimes in, "It's just a bunch of stuff that happened."

I find the idea of a world without meaning terrifying. I studied literature and continue to read indiscriminately and greedily, like I'm sinking and books are a lifeline. Literature provides reassurance that the world is not a meaningless place. It offers a mirror and a shield, a reflection of my own lived experience and a promise that our struggles matter. It offers lessons and morals, and when it doesn't, it offers the consolation that words can contain and shape, however briefly, the chaos, the messiness, and the pain of human existence.

But as much as I hate to acknowledge it, it's entirely possible that this is exactly what the world is: a place where a bunch of stuff just happens for no reason, and where, as Mara's preschool teacher liked to say, rather prosaically, "You get what you get and you don't throw a fit."

▶ Many of us have at least one issue or passion that we care deeply about—a topic on which we would love to share our opinions and insights in hopes of sparking intense interest and continued conversation. If you had ten minutes and the attention of a million people, what would your talk be about?

—USC

The Varsity Blues story breaks on March 12, 2019, and I start getting emails from a local television station, the *Wall Street Journal*, the *San Francisco Business Times* with requests for interviews.

I say no to all of them.

David, Jordan, and I are in New York City that week; Jordan is graduating from UOP at the end of May, and the trip is our graduation present to him. We're planning to gorge ourselves on bagels and pizza, to walk across the Brooklyn Bridge and stand atop iconic skyscrapers, to see a Yiddish-language production of *Fiddler on the Roof*, to wander through a massive exhibit of J. R. R. Tolkien's writings and illustrations at the Morgan Library, to visit the 9/11 Museum (through which Jordan will move slowly, reverently, asking questions, examining the artifacts, listening to the frantic voicemails, wondering out loud how people could do such things to each other).

David doesn't understand why I've turned down the interview requests. They would just take a few minutes, he says. National exposure, he says. I tell him I'm not remotely camera-ready (which is true; we've flown in that morning on a red-eye and I have bad hair and bags under my eyes), but there's more, and I can't quite put it into words. It's a feeling, not a reason—the scandal has laid bare the ugly underbelly of the need, the striving, the obsession with status and prestige that are the driving engine of my profession, and it feels like walking in on someone naked. I don't know what I could possibly say in an interview, how I can translate the churn of revulsion and pity and sadness into words. But I do know this: I don't want to parse or gloat or throw stones. I want to spend time with my husband and my son.

▶ Who in your life is depending on you? What are they depending on you for?

—UNIVERSITY OF TULSA

Mara hates Palo Alto. She says she can't wait to get out of here, that everyone is superficial and materialistic and obsessed with APs and internships and getting into Ivy League schools. She wants to go somewhere "real," like Colorado, and live in a van. The problem is that her transcript is full of B's and C's, she has not taken the SAT, and she has failed her behind the wheel test twice.[36] But Mara is nothing if not resourceful, and she finds a gap semester program in the South Pacific that offers college credit and—for students who maintain a B+ or better GPA—expedited admission to a number of colleges she likes, including University of Oregon and University of Vermont.

In August 2019, after a nerve-jangling sprint to the airport through rush-hour traffic because she didn't pack until the last minute, she goes to Fiji with a cohort of fifteen students from all over the United States; from there, they go

36. In February of her senior year, she screams at me and David that it's our fault she wasn't prepared to apply to college because we should have told her that the whole point of getting good grades was to get the fuck out of Palo Alto.

to New Zealand, and from there, to Australia. She comes back four months later, exuberant, full of plans and stories and a new confidence. She made friends; she helped prepare cassava with her host family; saw a cassowary, which almost attacked another girl in her group; she went to Hobbiton, which looks exactly like it does in the *Lord of the Rings* movies. She tells us about the vast differences in ways native people are treated in New Zealand and in Australia, and it seems like she's done it, she's gotten out of Palo Alto, and now it's on to college and independence and the darkness of high school is behind us.

But of course because nothing is easy for any of our children, it's not on to college and independence. The gap semester was a success socially but not academically; even though Mara started the semester with all A's, even though the work was easily within her ability and intelligence, she didn't turned her assignments in on time and didn't ask for help when she began struggling, and as a result, her GPA fell short of what she needed. Though she takes our suggestion and enrolls at the local community college to build up her GPA so she can transfer, either to one of the University of California campuses or to another college, that means she's stuck in Palo Alto.

And then the pandemic begins, and with it, the sense of a slowly moving apocalypse. Mara's classes move online. Noah, who gets a full-time job at Trader Joe's, moves out of our house and in with David's mom.[37] Jordan, who was living in the dorms at UOP and finishing his student teaching at a high school in Stockton, comes home after the campus shuts down. We alternate between lethargy and panic. My friend Tracy tells me she and her family exchange stories about nightmares they had every morning. I try to buy Sleepytime

37. David's mom is a saint.

tea and find that it's sold out everywhere, as is spray hair color to cover gray. And one day, while David is out running, I walk by Mara's room and hear a wheezing, gurgling sound, like she's snoring and choking at the same time, and I open the door and she's on her bed, unmoving and limp and blue around the lips, and when I pull her eyelids up, her eyes roll back in her head.

And because it's been twelve days since shelter-in-place, I think: *COVID*. I think: *respiratory arrest*. I do not think, *overdose*. And for the second time in five years I call 911 because one of my children is about to die.

The paramedics are much quicker on the uptake than I am. They give Mara a shot of Narcan and I wait in the hallway for endless molasses minutes and then I hear her voice and let out a breath I didn't know I was holding.

The Narcan makes Mara throw up, and the paramedics ask me to help her get changed before they take her to the ER. I find a pink sweatshirt with fumbling hands and try to help her into it, and we're both shaking, Mara because of the Narcan and me because she could have been dead had I not happened to pass by her room. She keeps saying, "I'm so sorry you had to see me like this," and I keep saying, "It's okay, you're going to be okay," because that's what you say when you're the mom, even if you don't believe a word of it.

And even though I'm pretty sure my heart can't be broken any more times, it fractures all over again when one of the paramedics asks, "Do you have any more of what you took?" and Mara nods yes and points to her bookshelf. Behind the books.

▶ Using a favorite quotation from an essay or book you have read in the last three years as a starting point, tell us about an event or experience that helped you define one of your values or changed how you approach the world. Please write the quotation, title and author at the beginning of your essay.

—PRINCETON UNIVERSITY

After great pain, a formal feeling comes—
The Nerves sit ceremonious, like Tombs—
The stiff Heart questions 'was it He, that bore,'
And 'Yesterday, or Centuries before'?

The Feet, mechanical, go round—
A Wooden way
Of Ground, or Air, or Ought—
Regardless grown,
A Quartz contentment, like a stone—

This is the Hour of Lead—
Remembered, if outlived,
As Freezing persons, recollect the Snow—
First—Chill—then Stupor—then the letting go—
—Emily Dickinson

The distance between the Redwood City Kaiser emergency room and our house is 7.7 miles, which translates into about 15,626 Fitbit steps, which I know because I walked it. I ride up front in the ambulance to the ER and then the paramedics wheel Mara into the ambulance bay and I walk around the building to the receptionist who tells me that no one is allowed in the hospital except patients and that someone will be in touch with more information. Don't call us, we'll call you. So I decide to walk home.

I could call David or Jordan for a ride, but I discard that thought as soon as it occurs to me. I want to walk, quickly and for a long time, without talking to anyone, without answering questions, wrapped in my mute, numb misery. And so I take Middlefield Road, which takes me through Redwood City, past taquerias and joyerias and storefronts with quinceañera dresses in ice cream colors. In Atherton, the sidewalk ends with almost no warning, and I walk on a dirt path on the shoulder under towering oaks, past palatial estates peeking out from behind tall stone walls. The sidewalk resumes in Menlo Park, winding its way through slightly less palatial estates, and then it's into Palo Alto. I cross University Avenue and walk past Lytton Gardens, where I used to meet Grandma Ester for our expeditions to Ross Dress for Less and Prolific Oven. The closer I get to home, the slower I walk. Walking is a solace; when I get to our front door, I'll have to stop. I will find a bewildered David, who has come back from his run to a house full of debris discarded by the paramedics. We will have to talk, to make plans, to figure out what to do next.

A lifetime ago, in my PhD oral exams, my dissertation advisor asked me to consider short and long forms—specifically, Emily Dickinson's twelve-line poem "After great pain, a formal feeling comes" in relation to Henry James's 545-page-long opus *The Portrait of a Lady*. At the time, this seemed like a particularly low blow; the question had been offered as one of several options on my written exam, and I chose a different one, and now here it was again, asked aloud at a seminar table in the Comparative Literature conference room, four other professors looking on with benign curiosity. This time, not optional. But after a brief, scrambling panic, I had it: Chapter 42, Isabel Archer's celebrated fireside vigil in her darkened drawing room as she considers her unhappy marriage. In the course of that still, silent contemplation, a storm rages in Isabel's mind. Carefully constructed convictions crumble, lurid flashes of lightning reveal her husband's monstrous egotism "curled like a serpent in a bank of flowers." Her belated realization that she had been played for a fool—had, in fact, unwittingly assisted in her own deception, had imagined "a world of things that had no substance"—crashes over her like a wave. The description of Isabel's solitary vigil, I said with growing confidence, echoes the numbness of the speaker in Emily Dickinson's poem, the profound sense of overwhelm and paralysis that comes on the heels of experiencing great pain. Dickinson's poem was written around 1862, nineteen years before *Portrait*, I continued (I had prepared well; the professors, even the treacherous Martha Banta, were nodding along), and how appropriate—whether or not James had actually read Dickinson—that this small form might be echoed in James's sprawling novel, where an entire drama, disorderly, violent, plays out within a single consciousness, followed by a great stillness.

This is the hour of lead, I keep thinking now. And then, *if outlived*. Who is the conditional for? Me? David? Mara? How much weight can a single person carry? (More weight, says Giles Corey in *The Crucible*.) And all the while I know, more certainly than I have ever known anything, that this weight, this darkness is not something I can outwalk, or outrun, or outthink.

▶ The University of Miami's official mascot is the ibis. Folklore maintains that the native marsh bird is the last to take shelter before a hurricane hits and the first to emerge once the storm passes, making it an apt symbol of courage and resilience.

Considering your ability to control your own motivation and behavior, how have past experiences helped build your courage and resilience to persist in the face of academic and life challenges so that, once these storms pass, you can emerge in continued pursuit of your goals?

—UNIVERSITY OF MIAMI

When our kids were little, we used to joke that as long as they were alive by the end of the day, we were doing a good job. I never imagined that there would come a time when keeping them alive would become an actual test of our parenting.

Our insurance plan places Mara into an intensive outpatient treatment program, which is all online because we're a month into quarantine. We discover that Mara almost died because she took a Xanax that, unbeknownst to her, was laced with fentanyl. The week after she overdoses, I see a short article in our local paper that two young people, twenty-two and twenty-four, died in nearly identical circumstances after taking fentanyl-laced OxyContin, and I suddenly understand Emily Dickinson's phrase, "zero at the bone," because I feel as though I've dropped through a sheet of ice into a frozen lake.

We discover that Mara had been self-medicating for anxiety and depression throughout high school and that she was using the *Diagnostic and Statistical Manual of Mental Disorders* to look up diagnostic criteria for various disorders so she could post about them on Tumblr (which encourages users to flaunt as many complex diagnoses as possible)—this in spite of the fact that her father is a psychiatrist and that she sees another psychiatrist for antidepressants (which she takes only sporadically) and goes to a therapist.

We discover that taking drugs and knowing about drugs was the only way she believed she could ever feel competent and in control. For all their horror, these discoveries feel like the lancing of an abscess. Knowing is agonizing but less terrifying than not knowing; now that it's out in the open, we can all confront it together.

The intensive outpatient program our insurance offers is 95 percent useless; it's followed by a stint at Aspiro, the same wilderness therapy program where we sent Jordan and Noah. Unlike her older brothers, who went more or less willingly, Mara fights us tooth and nail. She claims Aspiro did nothing to help either Jordan or Noah and screams at us and accuses us of taking away her autonomy and trying to control her, and I flash back to when she was three and a half and hell-bent on learning how to ride a bike, and whenever David or I tried to help she screamed, "I do it by self!" But this is not riding a bike, and our house is no longer safe for Mara. We tell her that she can choose not to go to Aspiro but can no longer live at home if she refuses, which is probably the most difficult thing we have ever had to say. Jordan stays in the background throughout all this, quiet and steady and unobtrusive; he tells Mara, who is frantic and desperate and wild-eyed, that he'll answer any questions she might have and that she can talk to him any time and we are too frantic and desperate and wild-eyed to properly appreciate the fact that Jordan is the one who knows exactly the right things to do and say. It's because of Jordan that we get Mara to the airport with less than thirteen minutes to spare before her flight to Utah.[38]

Mara is by far the most stubborn of our children, the one least likely to accept help or to even acknowledge that she needs it. Aspiro *did* help her, though not in the same way that it helped Jordan or Noah, and there is no resolution; she is currently on residential program number four, and we have no idea where her journey will take her, or us. But what I know is that we are lucky: lucky that she is alive, lucky that we can afford treatment when so many others cannot.

Still, there are times that I find myself thinking, *I did not sign up for this*. I did not sign up for neuropsych evaluations and endless parent interviews about whether my pregnancy was uneventful (yes, all three were, thank you) and conference calls and meetings with therapists, psychiatrists, placement specialists, and parent coaches. I did not sign up for the expense or the worry or despair or the guilt or the shame or the PTSD. I did not sign up for feeling defeated and depleted and helpless. I work with families whose children are second- or third-generation legacies at some of the most coveted colleges in the world. My kids? Well, we're now three for three at Aspiro Wilderness Adventures. At regular intervals, even: Jordan went in October of 2016, Noah went

38. Fun fact: it turns out that the Transportation Security Administration will let a passenger on a plane without an ID. (In a last-ditch bid to keep from going to Aspiro, Mara hid her passport in her room and claimed that she lost it, and we arrived at the airport with nothing but a ticket and her eleventh grade student ID from Paly. But when the plane is already boarding and you're nineteen and your destination is Utah and you're accompanied by a mother with tragic eyes, the TSA rep is likely to read between the lines and bend the rules.)

in June 2018, Mara went in September 2020. They give a 10 percent discount for younger siblings, so that's something.

There are days when I feel profoundly sorry for myself, and then I feel even worse about what any one of my children might be going through. There are days when everything feels miserable and hopeless. There are days when I wonder whether I'll ever wake up without a weight on my heart or a pit in my stomach. There are days that I'm convinced that people (I don't know who these people are, exactly, but that doesn't change the strength of my conviction) think of us with pity, or with horror, as the family with all the troubled children—or that my years of working to give other people's children what they wanted but didn't need made me incapable of giving my own children what they needed but didn't want.

I'm still working on acknowledging that our children have problems we can't solve on our own. I'm also perpetually on the lookout for the silver lining, if not the moral of the story, because this is how I think. In truth, our children's struggles and ours alongside them, as painful as they've been, have allowed us to understand and know each other in ways we might not have otherwise. We've done and experienced things other parents have not, and maybe our own suffering has given us a more generous, more compassionate view of the world.[39] What we've gone through has given me ways to measure success other than how it's measured in my line of work, and I sometimes find myself wondering about what might have happened if our children's lives had taken a different trajectory, had not wound through developmental delays, depression, anxiety, ADHD, substance abuse, wilderness therapy. Would we have become insufferable, smug people with a "proud parent of an honors student" bumper sticker and a

39. Which it totally has, but that doesn't mean I wouldn't snap my fingers and trade our hard-won wisdom for less painful lives for our children in a hot minute if that were possible.

narrow vision of what constitutes a successful life?

The families I work with come to me because they envision their child becoming a start-up founder, a doctor, a lawyer, a hedge fund manager, a VC, and I'm the conduit to get them there. They want the dream, which includes the decal of a prestigious college on the bumper of a prestigious car, ideally a late-model Tesla.[40] They want what David and I were when we were twenty-one, fresh out of college and headed to graduate school and med school and certain success.

When we moved into our crappy, overpriced house with single-pane windows that fogged up in the winter, we were prepared to live the dream. Advanced degrees, a piece of coveted Palo Alto real estate, safe streets, excellent schools. We, and our children, were going to be successful—successful by conventional measures, that is. Successful as in high school → college → white collar job. Successful in the way David and I were successful. Successful as in deserving *and* lucky.

Let's face it: in the drama of our own lives, we all want to be both deserving and lucky. We want to be Odysseus, not the suitors; Cinderella, not the stepsisters; Charlie Bucket, not Veruca Salt or Augustus Gloop. And then David and I became parents, and parenthood undid us. It left us bruised and battered and humbled. It taught us things about ourselves we would have preferred not to know: that we were flawed, that we were vain, that we cared more about what others thought than was probably healthy, that we sometimes sought refuge in work, which felt easier than parenting three children we couldn't understand. But we also learned how fiercely we were capable of loving, how hard we were willing to fight, how deeply proud we would be of their victories, large as well as small.

---

40. I should note here that until fairly recently I drove a 1999 Toyota Sienna with a big dent in the rear bumper, a missing passenger-side door handle, and a driver's-side window that would sometimes slide all the way up and sometimes not. There's a metaphor here somewhere.

Recently, Mara's therapist asked us to read Brad Reedy's *The Journey of the Heroic Parent*,[41] and either because we were ready to hear it or because the other books about parenting struggling kids are mostly crap (I suspect mostly the latter), this one actually makes all kinds of sense. It suggests setting aside outcome-based parenting and holding your children's failures and successes loosely. Which I take to mean that your children may take flight or they may not, but they are more likely to fly unweighted by the ballast of expectations.

41. I want to be clear: David and I don't consider ourselves heroic parents. We've simply dealt with what we've had to deal with, like the ibis (which is neither heroic nor unheroic, neither courageous nor cowardly, but just a bird doing bird things).

▶ We know you lead a busy life, full of activities, many of which are required of you. Tell us about something you do simply for the pleasure of it.

—MIT

If it weren't for improv, I'm pretty sure David and I would have lost our minds a long time ago.

David signs us up for a one-time improv comedy for beginners class after Jordan goes to UOP, and what begins as a lark quickly turns into a minor obsession. Our teacher is a big teddy bear of a man who wears T-shirts with flying cats and rainbow suspenders and is relentlessly enthusiastic without being the least bit fake or weird about it. The other students range from tech people our age who have signed up for improv to be more effective communicators at work to a Stanford student to a middle school math teacher with a wicked sense of humor. The twelve of us meet every Wednesday at 7:00 p.m. in a bare room at Cubberley Community Center; we start with basic improv games like "Zip Zap Zop" and "I Am a Tree" and gradually progress to storytelling games like "String of Pearls," where you step up to tell a story one sentence at a time in random order without having the slightest idea of what the story actually is because you're all making it up as you go along. In one story, "and she never went outside again" is the last sentence and the sentence "and all night long, the dogs were barking" is somewhere in the middle, and it's unclear to all of us what is happening until the middle school math teacher steps up to the beginning of the line, poker-faced, and says, "Once upon a time, there was a girl who wore a dress made of meat," and we all double over laughing.

To do improv is to become intimately familiar with failure. In fact, the first thing we learn is the clown bow, which is when you step into the middle of a circle, throw your hands up exuberantly, and proclaim as loudly and confidently as you can, "I failed!"—and in response, your classmates whoop and clap and holler in approval. We play games called "brain fries," deliberately designed to mess with your head, to short-circuit your thinking, to make you blurt out the wrong thing, until slowly we start to realize that blurting out the wrong thing is sort of the point. One of my favorite games is played in groups of two: you or your partner start a story, one sentence at a time, and the person listening is supposed to say, "and then what happens?" after each sentence if they want the storyteller to continue. If the listener doesn't like the direction of the story or has a different idea, they say, "Nope" in a pleasantly neutral voice, and the roles reverse; the previous storyteller asks, "and then what happens?" and the new storyteller takes over. I love the give-and-take of it, the fact that no one is in charge of a story, that things can turn and pivot at any moment, usually toward some kind of nonsense or hilarity or both.

Improv teaches us to listen closely, to make our partner look good instead of worrying about whether *we're* any good, to say "yes," to reconcile concepts that have no place being in the same story, let alone in the same room. In spite—or, perhaps because of—the fact that we both make a living talking and giving advice and thinking on the fly,

David and I struggle with these concepts. We have a hard time staying in the moment, thinking only one sentence ahead, and not worrying about how we're doing or whether others are judging us. When we graduate to doing scenes, we feel wooden and clumsy. But we stick with it, because occasionally we catch a glimpse of what improv competence might look like—that is, when we're not bathed in flop sweat thinking frantically about our character's motivation, location, or objective or about how to convincingly mime toasting bread, which is called space object work.

There is a magic in creating a story or a scene from nothing, with only an audience suggestion to go on. In one class, David stands up to do a scene that he starts by morosely carrying an invisible dead cat, and our teacher stops him and says, "Now do the same thing, but be super excited about it," and David walks off and bounces into the scene yelling gleefully, "I found a dead cat!" and his scene partner, without missing a beat, says, "Cool, another one!" It turns out that the two of them are amateur taxidermists who have been collecting roadkill. And that is how we learn about the importance of a positive attitude, of starting a scene "happy, healthy, fit."

Improv helps when our life feels like a series of biblical plagues—like, we've already had the near-death of the firstborn and the youngest, so bring on the darkness at noon, the locusts, the kitchen faucet running with blood. Improv gives us a place to go for three hours each week, and in that place it's okay not to know what's going to happen next.

Friends of ours who don't get it ask us if we're taking improv to "improve our marriage, ha ha." We are not. Our marriage is fine, actually. We do it to remind ourselves that it's okay to suck at something and that anything is possible. Sometimes you just have to put on the meat dress. To swing the bedraggled corpse of a cat over your shoulder, but with glee this time.

▶ As you look into the future, what gives you hope?

—ELON UNIVERSITY

Three months after Mara's overdose, the pear tree in our back yard that has not yielded a single pear for ten years suddenly begins bearing fruit.

During quarantine, Noah, who has worked at Trader Joe's steadily for a year and a half, starts bringing us groceries and throwing in an occasional container of dark chocolate peanut butter cups or saddle chips, which are like Pringles but better. He still doesn't see himself going to college, but he talks about unionizing Trader Joe's employees and potentially running for public office. We're learning to listen more and talk less when we speak with him; when he complains about his job, we don't say, "Maybe you should have stayed in college," even though we want to with every fiber of our being. We nod and say, "That must be hard."

Mara has started reading again; she even tries *Anna Karenina*, though she gives up after a while. I don't always love her choice of books (she adores Gillian Flynn's *Gone Girl* and *Sharp Objects*) but I don't tell her that. In a recent conversation, she tells us she's thinking about majoring in English and folklore when she goes to college.

Jordan completed his student teaching in 2020 and is about to set off for his first teaching job at an under-resourced school in San Diego, which is exactly what he wanted because he believes in inclusion and equity. As I write, he is making lists—a list of essentials he's planning to bring with him and a list called "contingency plans for unexpected occurrences."

A few months ago, he dug up an old Star Wars cookbook and announced that he was going to make Bossk Brownies, which is a recipe an average ten-year-old can make with minimal adult supervision, but because Jordan is neither an average ten-year-old nor an average adult, the brownie-making is a disaster. He can't find the measuring spoons or the bowls. He spills cocoa powder into the flour canister and dribbles raw egg on the kitchen counter and one of our cats knocks over the container of baking powder and Jordan loses it and shouts that he can't do anything, even make a kid recipe, and that this is just bullshit. Then David steps in and talks to him quietly and together they salvage the brownie situation and stick the pan in the oven and forty-three minutes later the brownies emerge and they are delicious. And after we compliment him, Jordan smiles shyly and says yeah, it was really hard but totally worth it.

▶ What is the truest thing you know? How did you come to this conclusion?

—VILLANOVA

Dear Rising Senior,

Listen up: Arnold Spirit Junior from *The Absolutely True Diary of a Part-Time Indian* is getting in and you're not, even though he's fictional and you're real. Why? Because you're googling things like "how do you get into a highly selective college" and he lives on the rez with bullies, an alcoholic father, and more heartbreak than you will experience over the course of your entire life. And yeah, you are actually the lucky one, because even though he's getting in and you're not, he doesn't have parents who can pay full freight for four years at a private college. He never had tutors or SAT prep classes or $120 sneakers for just kicking around. But it's so stressful to be you, you protest. It's not fair. This kid has natural gifts: he's bright, a talented graphic artist, and a member of an underrepresented minority. You play trumpet in the school band and have mostly A's and an engineer dad and doctor mom who drive you to the local community college where you're taking statistics to boost your GPA and nothing exciting ever happens to you.

Speaking of exciting things that have happened to other people, here's who else, fictional as well as real, would get into a highly selective college: Anne Frank; Scout Finch; the creature in *Frankenstein* (who faced a *lot* of adversity and who will probably be too busy prowling the North Pole to attend college even if admitted); Mary Shelley, who wrote *Frankenstein* when she was eighteen and had already run away from home and had two children and a miscarriage by then; Jane Eyre; Bertha Mason, the madwoman in the attic, will be too (it would be funny if she and Jane were assigned to the same dorm); Marie-Laure Leblanc in *All the Light We Cannot See*; Pi, from *Life of Pi*; Huck Finn; Charlie Bucket, duh; Alice in *Through the Looking-Glass*; Sasha Goldberg in *Petropolis*; Emily Dickinson, probably, but I'm guessing she wouldn't go.

I am not trying to rub it in. I am simply a little bird with a message. I should also point out that there are well over 2,500 colleges that would be delighted to admit a teenager who has not taken a dozen college-level classes before graduating from high school; fled political repression; navigated the world entirely alone, rejected by everyone; fallen down rabbit holes; invented anything; or sheltered fugitives. But you don't want any of them, do you? You want the top ten, maybe the top twenty, if you're feeling expansive. Maybe you'll "even" go to Berkeley, as a student once told me he might do if Harvard and Columbia don't work out.

How do I know all this? I read a lot of books as a kid, and then I majored in English, and then I got a PhD, and then I taught literature and composition to college freshmen before working for four years in the admissions office of a highly selective university. Precious few spots are available for anyone, even the geniuses, even the kids with extraordinary, wrenching stories, like the gay Hispanic student who kept her sexual orientation hidden from her family but confided it to us, the nameless, faceless admission readers, or the student who watched the Pentagon burn on 9/11 not knowing whether his father, who was inside, was alive or dead. Suburban kids who have all their limbs and straight A's and SAT scores in the 98th percentile and who have done 100 hours of community service—heck, even 500, which qualifies you for the President's Award? Yeah, not so much.

For the past fifteen years, I've worked as an independent college consultant. Every fall, I help students figure out how to tell their best story—how to find the germ of a good idea in what is often an uneventful life dutifully devoted to all the suburban markers of success: sports teams, bands, science competitions, speech and debate competitions, math competitions, an endless parade of tutors, summer enrichment programs, volunteering at the Boys and Girls Club, volunteering in Tanzania, volunteering in Nicaragua, volunteering at the local soup kitchen. Occasionally I get a kid who breaks the mold and does something unusual—a girl who haunts the local thrift store, buys ugly old dresses, rips them up and remakes them in a jaunty '40s style, with oversized buttons and flounces and ruched sleeves; a boy whose family lives near a Louisiana swamp where he performs research on a rare microbe in the local ecosystem; another boy who bakes extravagant desserts and helps with outreach at a free clinic in San Francisco every weekend. Those essays practically write themselves. But a lot of the time, I have to dissuade the soccer player from writing about how his ACL surgery inspired him to want to become a doctor or discourage an essay about volunteering in a developing country and making meaningful eye contact with an emaciated child on the street. (But the child smiled at me, the student tells me. In spite of being emaciated and covered in sores and standing ankle-deep in sewage! Because poor people lead such simple, pure lives!)

And don't get me started on your parents—parents who use HYPS as a synecdoche for highly selective schools, who talk about "packaging" and "messaging" and "positioning" as though you were a product ready for launch, parents who second- and third-guess everything, who are riddled with anxiety and angst, who worry that you don't have a "spark," who want what's best for you but who also want bragging rights come April of your senior year. It's enough to drive you to drink. (Me, that is; you're still underage.) It's certainly enough to drive anyone to become cynical and bitter. Come November of each application season, when the anxiety is high and deadlines loom, I start to feel like the female version of Dostoyevsky's Underground Man—cantankerous, bitter, petty. Once, while listening to a student struggle to identify five words to describe herself for the Stanford application, I scrawled five of my own on a Post-it note to describe myself: spiteful, grammatical, grudge-holding short lady.

In spite of all my rancor, I love working with teenagers—I really do—especially when the barbed anxiety of HYPS is not on the table. They're full of ideas and questions and an intense, fizzy energy. They remind me of my younger, unrealized, yearning self. As a college freshman, I proudly displayed books on my bookshelf that I thought would add to my intellectual cachet (the collected poems of E. E. Cummings, *The Master and Margarita*—in two translations *and* the original Russian—*The Metamorphosis*, *Rosencrantz and Guildenstern Are Dead*, *Waiting for Godot*). And, okay, I judged, and still judge, people (in my head, though, not usually out loud) who confuse "your" and "you're," who are incurious, who shrug and say, "I don't really like to read." These days, particularly when I'm cranky, I judge students for all of the above plus (again, silently) for being concrete and obtuse in their thinking about college and what it means, like when they say, "If I take AP Biology *and* become president of Key Club, would I get into Stanford?"

You will *not* get into Stanford if you pursue that line of questioning. The students I've seen get into Stanford are usually too busy being extraordinary to care whether they get into Stanford or not. Nobody needs to get into Stanford, but it does help to stretch yourself, and not necessarily by taking all the AP classes you can get your hands on. You might be extraordinarily kind, like the girl who spent two years in a senior home teaching the residents how to use Facebook and Instagram to connect with their digital-native grandchildren because she realized that her own grandmother was desperately lonely. Or extraordinarily brilliant, like the kid who patented an invention that converted something into something else. (Confession: I don't even get half of what my students do, especially the STEM kids, but I can tell by the hair standing up on the back of my neck who's extraordinary. It's one of my savant skills, in addition to knowing how to cut a 300-word paragraph into 150 words while keeping its essence and style intact.) Extraordinarily talented. Extraordinarily small, like the boy who weighed 110 pounds soaking wet and discovered that he could be a coxswain (a word he didn't even know how to spell as a ninth grader) after striking out, spectacularly, in every other sport. Sometimes, you just have to have the good luck to be born into an extraordinarily rich family. Yes, that means that the bland, barely competent children of billionaires will sometimes be admitted, and you won't be. Some of them are actually not all that bland, and not all of them, in spite of what you'd assume, are smug and entitled. Some of them are anguished and troubled by the weight of money and privilege that hangs on their fragile shoulders. The girls especially remind me of Henry James's tragic heiresses—Maggie Verver, Milly Theale, Isabel Archer. They decide that they don't want to apply Early Decision to Brown, even though they're a double legacy at Brown, going back two generations on the mom's side, because they want to go to art school, and no, not RISD. And then there will be extensive, operatic, high-level negotiations between parent and child, me and child, me and parent, about What To Do.

At staff training my first year reading at Stanford, the dean of admission asked the assembled admission officers if we thought we could get into Stanford if we applied today. And I thought to myself: I sure as hell couldn't (and didn't) when I was seventeen, but I sure as hell could if I applied that day. Why? Because I'd learned how to tell a story, to spy the barely there silken thread of narrative trailing into the foliage and brambles of everyday experience. Because I'd lived and suffered. Because I'd learned that things are rarely what they appear to be—both for good and ill.

When I applied at seventeen, I was superficial and stupid. I drew a self-portrait in one of the supplemental essay spaces of my application, and my mother looked over my shoulder and asked, "Are you supposed to do that?" and I rolled my eyes and said, "They'll think I'm creative, *Mom.*" (Reader, they did not.) If I had a do-over, I would have written about trying to translate Bulgakov's *The Master and Margarita* in my junior year. But at the time, I didn't think that was college essay–worthy, because after doing a passable job with Chapter 1, where Berlioz and Bezdomny, a Soviet literary editor and an up-and-coming poet, meet a mysterious foreigner on the outskirts of Moscow, I gave up one paragraph into Chapter 2, defeated by the impossible stylistic shift from quotidian prose to the incantatory, majestic cadences of the scene in which Christ, called Yeshua Ha-Notsri in the novel, and Pontius Pilate meet for the first time. And that's the thing: most seventeen-year-olds don't realize that failing in an ambitious undertaking—and delving into the reasons for failing—is far more interesting than succeeding.

I also didn't know that the translated first chapter and my pathetic attempt at the first paragraph of the second chapter would lead me to meet Michael Heim my freshman year at UCLA, where I had gone grudgingly because no other schools except Boston University would have me and my 3.3 GPA and my parents refused to pay for BU. Michael Heim, who picked up languages like some people pick up a handful of peanuts from a bowl on the bar, was one of the most brilliant and renowned Slavic translators in the world, and I had no idea that he taught at UCLA or that he would see something in those four frayed inexpertly typed pages marred with white-out and penciled-in revisions, and that as a result I would have my first adult—professional—conversation about the technical and stylistic aspects of translation. We spent over an hour in his narrow, book-jammed office, the light from the tall, narrow window behind him lighting his messy collar-length hair and his angular face with the jutting jaw and his Lincoln-like beard. After that conversation he took me under his wing and encouraged me to go to graduate school and to study comparative literature and suggested writing about Vladimir Nabokov and Henry James, two American authors who weren't really American. That offhand suggestion would become my dissertation, *The Question of Their Speech: Plotting Exile in the Life and Work of Henry James and Vladimir Nabokov*, which I wrote as my firstborn son, Jordan, who would be diagnosed with high-functioning autism at age two, was failing to develop meaningful speech of any kind.

My dissertation would lead me to my first post-PhD job, a lectureship at Stanford, which would lead me to a stint at the admission office, which would lead me to what I do now, even in my monstrously bifurcated world. There's a lot you don't know when you're seventeen, so that's my job: to see the order in the chaos; to spy the story, the twist, the interesting thing in the thicket of everyday experience; to show you that everything is connected; to help you see how life makes ornaments from accidents and possibilities; to give you the long view you don't have yet. Your parents look at me beseechingly, willing me to make you stand out from the crowd, to make you extraordinary, but if you're a garden-variety average excellent kid, I can no more do that than I could make my oldest son not autistic, or his younger brother not apathetic, or their younger sister not anxious or depressed. What I can do is try to help you understand who you are and to find the right words to tell your story.

For I am still obsessed with stories. I am a sucker for narrative symmetry, for the snake-biting-its-tail ending (ouroboros, if you want to know the technical term), in literature and in life. I dig around, compulsively, for the beginnings and ends of things, for the small, insignificant-seeming detail that might lead to a revelatory truth, that might allow you to glimpse the extraordinary in the ordinary. If you're brainstorming an essay with me, I will ask you how you became interested in coding, why you picked water polo and not swimming, what it's like to live with your non-English speaking grandmother from India who moved in five years ago, about the koi pond your grandfather dug with his own hands in his backyard, about your obsession with the Marvel universe, about the stupid reality show you watch religiously every week with your younger sister. Your parents shake their heads and wonder if those are stories—trivial, inconsequential—that admissions officers want to hear. They write me emails late at night wondering if it would be better to write about being treasurer of the French Club or that summer you spent in Honduras.

Believe me, nobody cares about your being treasurer of the French Club, unless you embezzled money from the croissant fundraiser or something. That would be a good story, though not a good way to get into college. Honduras might be okay, as long as you don't write about the happy poor people. Please don't write about the happy poor people and their idyllic, simple lives.

Instead, be alert to the intricate web of connections that's all around you. Getting into a highly selective college is, frankly, not all that interesting. There are other paths, some of them frightening, some of them tragic, some of them exhilarating. They may wind through college, or they may not. *The Master and Margarita*, that book I tried to translate and never finished? I once recommended it to a lost, purposeless kid who was smoking pot daily and flunking out of community college but evinced a passing interest in Russian culture and politics, never thinking he'd actually read it. Three years later, I heard from his mom: after finishing it, he took intensive Russian language classes at the Naval Postgraduate School in Monterey, became nearly fluent, then became a freelance correspondent based in Tbilisi, Georgia, for *The Daily Beast*, reported on the 2014 Russian invasion of Crimea, and was then admitted as a transfer student to Columbia. Yes, that Columbia. The highly selective one. My point is, he was a lot of things before he was a Columbia student, and by the time he applied, he didn't need Columbia; Columbia needed him.

And then there was this. Five or so years ago, I was driving home from an appointment with a student—earnest, hardworking, desperate to do all the right things to get into a "good" college, paralyzed by anxiety that nothing he had done, would ever do, would be good enough—I heard a story on NPR: "Police are investigating the discovery of a human foot that washed up on a San Francisco beach earlier today near Taraval St. There is no sign of a body. The foot, clad in a Puma running shoe, appears to have spent some time in a seabed before washing ashore."

And because I studied English and read Shakespeare, I immediately thought of Ariel's song to Ferdinand in *The*

Tempest: "Full fathom five thy father lies / Of his bones are coral made / Those are pearls that were his eyes / Nothing of him that doth fade / But doth suffer a sea-change / Into something rich and strange."

And as I was thinking all this, the announcer specified that the shoe was green and black mesh, size 11½—just to make everything that much more ghastly—and I thought, again, *There are some things you just can't outrun.* But then wasn't it Nietzsche, or maybe Camus, who said that we have art in order not to perish from the truth?

The student I had seen that day committed suicide several years later, as a college junior, to all appearances accomplished, handsome, popular. To this day I wonder if the NPR story about the foot in the Puma running shoe was a portent, if I should have done anything differently, if I should have been more aggressive in making more of a point that getting into college—any college—is not the beginning or the end of anything. It's just another plot point.

All good stories—tragedy and comedy both—are all about what *isn't* supposed to happen, and about what happens after *that*. It's the knot in the rope, the irritation in the oyster, the disruption that drives narratives forward. It's the plot of everything from *The Odyssey* to *Unbreakable Kimmy Schmidt*. Cinderella is not supposed to go to the ball. Isabel is not supposed to marry Osmond. Bluebeard's wife isn't supposed to open the door. Oedipus . . . well, he actually does do what he's supposed to do, but only because he's trying so hard not to do it.

So all those people—fictional and real—I mentioned earlier? People who would probably get into a college of their choice even if they had mediocre SATs or a bad transcript (or no transcript, because they were marooned, or in hiding, or on the run, which made regular school attendance difficult)? The funny thing is that they're not even trying to get in. College is probably the last thing on their mind. Mostly, they're just trying to survive and not, you know, starve to death or be captured by Nazis or get beaten to death by their drunken dad or eaten by a tiger who is sharing a raft with them. (Do you notice, by the way, how many of them are on boats or rafts? Or confined to attics?)

And yet they've all lived, richly, fully, audaciously. They *could* be admitted to a highly selective college, but they have bigger fish to fry (speaking of which, Ishmael would definitely be admitted; Ahab, probably not). And you will live, too, if you let yourself. We all come into the world by accident, we will very likely leave it by accident, but in between—in what Virginia Woolf called the brief season between two silences—there is more than accident. There is volition. There is intent. You will go out into the world, and things will happen to you, but you will also *do* things, and make things happen, and you will (I hope) no longer care about your GPA or class rank or SAT scores or whether your résumé shows sufficient leadership because you will be too busy living and doing. And later, when you look back on the loopy, recursive non-logic of unfolding events, you'll see a pattern so intricate it will make your head hurt to contemplate the coincidences and complex twists and turns that led to its making, to its obvious inevitability. It might strike you as ugly, or dazzlingly beautiful, or some improbable combination of the two. But I promise you that the astonishing truth of it will smack you in the head and you will say, "Wow. Wow. You can't make this shit up."

Nabokov wrote in the afterword to *Lolita* that for him, a work of fiction existed "only insofar as it affords me what I shall bluntly call aesthetic bliss, that is a sense of being somehow, somewhere, connected with other states of being where art (curiosity, tenderness, kindness, ecstasy) is the norm." Probably because I miss teaching, and being in Nabokov's curmudgeonly, brilliant company as I wrote about him in my dissertation, I unconsciously end up paraphrasing that quote in follow-up reports about students who desperately want to go to Stanford, Harvard, Princeton, Yale, or other schools that they, or their equally desperate, hopeful, striving parents designate "top notch." Because the fact that their chances of getting into those schools hover between zero and one percent is too depressing to contemplate at length, I always make sure to include a line in the follow-up reports that goes like this: "There are hundreds of other colleges and universities where a student with imagination, curiosity, creativity, and a willingness to work hard will thrive."

This might sound like I'm handing out a consolation prize, and I am, sort of, but it also happens to be true. There's a whole universe out there, a universe independent of your alma mater, a universe of the imagination that Nabokov called "unreal estate." Even if you're not at your dream college, even if you're in a place you hate, even if you're discouraged and despairing, that universe—invisible, democratic, all-embracing, catholic—is right there for the taking. It's a state of being that I aspire to every day. I hope I get in. I hope we all do.

WORKS REFERENCED:

Aeschylus, *The Oresteia*
Aristotle, *Nicomachean Ethics*
Honoré de Balzac, *Père Goriot*
Charles Blow, "The Passion of Parenting," *New York Times*, Nov. 6, 2013
Charlotte Bronte, *Jane Eyre*
Mikhail Bulgakov, *The Master and Margarita*
Geoffrey Chaucer, *The Miller's Tale*
Shirley Conran, *Lace*
Roald Dahl, *Charlie and the Chocolate Factory*
Emily Dickinson, poems
T. S. Eliot, *The Wasteland*
Howard Fast, *The Immigrants, Second Generation*
William Faulkner, *Absalom, Absalom!*
Nathaniel Hawthorne, *The Scarlet Letter*
Homer, *The Odyssey*
Henry James, *The Portrait of a Lady*
Rudyard Kipling, *Just So Stories*, "If"
Judith Krantz, *Mistral's Daughter, Scruples*
Herman Melville, *Moby-Dick*
Toni Morrison, *Sula*

Vladimir Nabokov, *Lolita, Pale Fire, Strong Opinions, The Gift*
Aleksandr Pushkin, *The Tale of Tsar Saltan*
Brad Reedy, *The Journey of the Heroic Parent*
David Sedaris, "Season's Greetings to Our Friends and Family!!!"
William Shakespeare, *The Tempest, King Lear*
Mary Shelley, *Frankenstein*
George Steiner, *Extraterritorial*
J. R. R. Tolkien, *The Hobbit, The Lord of the Rings*
Leo Tolstoy, *Anna Karenina*
Leon Uris, *Exodus, Mila-18*
Maksimilian Voloshin, poems
Walt Whitman, "I Sing the Body Electric"
Virginia Woolf, *To the Lighthouse*
Herman Wouk, *The Winds of War*

ACKNOWLEDGMENTS

Most books have complicated birth stories. Mine starts in the late 1970s, when I met and became friends with Lilya Kaganovsky, who came to the US from the Soviet Union at roughly the same time as I did and who, when we were in high school, encouraged my early attempts at satirical nonfiction by peering over my shoulder and snickering appreciatively as I chronicled a now legendary multi-family, multi-state road trip in my spiral notebook. Years later, after we became mature and dignified adults, Lilya introduced me to her friend Caroline Grant, who subsequently became my friend and a cherished fellow traveler in the creative nonfiction universe; many years after *that*, Caroline introduced me to Nicki Richesin (thereby becoming this book's honorary godmother). Nicki took a chance on me even though I had no clue what a book proposal was, made incredibly insightful suggestions that transformed a disheveled collection of vignettes into a coherent manuscript, persisted through 60+ rejections with superhuman patience and optimism, and introduced me to Brooke Warner at She Writes Press. I am deeply grateful to all of these phenomenally talented, generous women as well as to the She Writes editorial and design teams—Samantha Strom, Krissa Lagos, Tabitha Lahr, and Lindsey Cleworth—whose collective vision helped shepherd this book into the world.

I also owe an enormous debt of gratitude to the following people:

Laurie Filipelli, my spiritual twin, who encouraged me to keep writing, traded stories about indomitable grandmothers, and sent me poems and Randy Rainbow videos when things got bleak.

Elyse Fenton, who, to borrow from Jeanette Winterson, understands how words work in the same way that some people understand how car engines work. I can't begin to do justice to her generous, exacting, gimlet-eyed editing.

Katherine Ellison, who was a champion of this book when it was still a murky glimmer at the end of a very long tunnel.

Stacey Lorinczi, Nanci Pass, Tracy Stewart, Diane Sussman, and Jeny Wegbreit, who listened, cheered, fed me, helped me see both the forest and the trees, and walked with me through forests and trees, literal and metaphorical.

The teachers, counselors, therapists, and friends who saw our children—really saw them—and were kind, even when it wasn't easy.

The many families who have trusted their children to me and who showed me that parenting comes in many forms.

The many students whose stories I will always treasure.

My parents, who when I was in middle school gave me a globe for my birthday and made a joke about giving me the world and I was mad because what fun is a globe except now I realize that they really did give me the world. Thank you.

David Smith, who asked to be described as a handsome and successful physician, and who is that and so much more, has been a cheerleader, a talker-off-the-ledge, an extravagantly patient reader, a web design genius, an amateur cover designer, a purveyor of take-out and common sense, and my best friend.

And last, but absolutely not least, my three extraordinary, rampageous children—Jordan, Noah, and Mara—who have astonished me, challenged me, made me laugh, and taught me more than they will ever know. You are all *taps heart* right here.

ABOUT THE AUTHOR

Irena Smith was born in the former Soviet Union and grew up in Moscow in the waning days of the Brezhnev regime; in 1977, her family emigrated from the USSR and sought asylum in the United States as political refugees. She has been published in *HIAS@130: 1+30: The Best of myStory, Mama, PhD: Women Write about Motherhood and Academic Life, Literary Mama*, and *Art in the Time of Unbearable Crisis*. She has a PhD in comparative literature from UCLA and lives in Palo Alto, California.

SELECTED TITLES FROM SHE WRITES PRESS

She Writes Press is an independent publishing company founded to serve women writers everywhere. Visit us at www.shewritespress.com.

Poetic License: A Memoir by Gretchen Eberhart Cherington. $16.95, 978-1-63152-711-1. At age forty, with two growing children and a consulting company she'd recently founded, Gretchen Cherington, daughter of Pulitzer Prize–winning poet Richard Eberhart, faced a dilemma: Should she continue to silence her own voice? Or was it time to speak her truth—even the unbearable truth that her generous and kind father had sexually violated her?

Not a Poster Child: Living Well with a Disability—A Memoir by Francine Falk-Allen. $16.95, 978-1631523915. Francine Falk-Allen was only three years old when she contracted polio and temporarily lost the ability to stand and walk. Here, she tells the story of how a toddler learned grown-up lessons too soon; a schoolgirl tried her best to be a "normie," on into young adulthood; and a woman finally found her balance, physically and spiritually.

Blinded by Hope: One Mother's Journey Through Her Son's Bipolar Illness and Addiction by Meg McGuire. $16.95, 978-1-63152-125-6. A fiercely candid memoir about one mother's roller coaster ride through doubt and denial as she attempts to save her son from substance abuse and bipolar illness.

Dearest Ones at Home: Clara Taylor's Letters from Russia, 1917-1919 edited by Katrina Maloney and Patricia Maloney. $18.95, 978-1-63152-931-3. Clara Taylor's detailed, delightful letters documenting her two years in Russia teaching factory girls self-sufficiency skills—right in the middle of World War I.

The Odyssey and Dr. Novak: A Memoir by Ann C. Colley. $16.95, 978-1-63152-343-4. Recalling personal experiences of living in Warsaw and Kiev, Ann C. Colley creates a complex, composite portrait of Poland and Ukraine at a time between the fall of the Soviet Union and the recent resurgence of a Russian threat.

Indestructible: The Hidden Gifts of Trauma by Krista Nerestant. $16.95, 978-1-63152-799-9. Krista Nerestant endured multiple traumas as a child in the Philippines and a young immigrant in the United States—yet she rose to face every obstacle she encountered with courage and self-love. Along the way, she found success and healing, discovered the hidden gifts of trauma, and eventually became a spiritual medium and inspirational leader in her community.